Decem

Also by Richard Hugo

A Run of Jacks

Death of the Kapowsin Tavern

Good Luck in Cracked Italian

The Lady in Kicking Horse Reservoir

What Thou Lovest Well Remains American

31 Letters and 13 Dreams

Selected Poems

White Center

The Right Madness on Skye

Making Certain It Goes On: The Collected Poems of Richard Hugo

The Real West Marginal Way: A Poet's Autobiography
(edited by Ripley Hugo, Lois Welch, and James Welch)

THE

TRIGGERING

TOWN

Lectures and Essays

on Poetry and Writing

The
TRIGGERING
TOWN

Lectures and Essays

on Poetry and Writing

by Richard Hugo

W · W · NORTON & COMPANY

New York · London

Printed in the United States of America.
All Rights Reserved
First published as a Norton paperback 1982; reissued 1992
Library of Congress Cataloging in Publication Data
Hugo, Richard F   /   The triggering town.
1. Poetics—Addresses, essays, lectures.
2. Authorship—Addresses, essays, lectures. I. Title.
PN1042.H8   808.1   78-26031

ISBN 0-393-30933-9

W. W. Norton & Company, Inc.
500 Fifth Avenue, New York, N.Y. 10110
W. W. Norton & Company Ltd
10 Coptic Street, London WC1A 1PU

2 3 4 5 6 7 8 9 0

ACKNOWLEDGEMENTS

Some of these chapters have appeared as follows:

"Assumptions"—*Northwest Review*

"How Poets Make a Living"—*Iowa Review*

"Ci Vediamo"—*Slackwater Review*

"Statements of Faith"—*Atlantic Monthly*

"Stray Thoughts on Roethke and Teaching," "The Triggering Town," "Writing off the Subject," "In Defense of Creative Writing Classes," and "Nuts and Bolts"—*American Poetry Review*

The author wishes to thank the University of
Montana Foundation for its support while he was
writing one of the chapters of this book

For all students of creative writing

—and for their teachers

Contents

❧

Introduction

પ

THIS BOOK contains lectures, essays, and a couple of sentimental reminiscences. I trust they all relate to problems of writing. This is not intended as a textbook, though it is true I teach creative writing to make my living, and I am trying to reproduce some of the things I do in the classroom. Most of the material here I teach to students in beginning poetry-writing classes, usually college freshmen and sophomores. Some of the material, however, I use in more advanced courses.

Many writers and many writing teachers believe reading and writing have a close and important relationship. Over the years I have come to doubt this. Like many others, I once believed that by study one could discover and ingest some secret ingredient of literature that later would find its way into one's own work. I've come to believe that one learns to write only by writing. Years ago in the comic strip "Pogo," a bear appeared, a creature who could write but couldn't read. Granted the joke, I'm not sure anymore that the concept is that farfetched. I'm inclined more and more to believe that writing, like sex, is psychogenic, though I could probably be argued out of it.

I'm not trying to undermine the study and teaching of literature. Far from it. I think literature should be studied for the most serious of all reasons: it is fun. For a young writer it should be exciting as well.

I believe that a writer learns from reading possibilities of technique, ways of execution, phrasing, rhythm, tonality, pace. Otherwise, reading is important if it excites the imagination, but what excites the imagination may be found in any number of experiences (or in a lack of them). Reading may or may not be one. I can think of four current writers, three of them poets, whose work stimulates me to write. I've seen dozens of triggering towns.

If I had to sum up my way of helping others to write poems, and I hope you if you are just starting, I'd say that I try as seldom as I can to talk about a newly offered poem from the standpoint of the reader. Instead, if I can, I talk as if I'd written the poem myself and try to find out why and where I went wrong. Obviously this is a limited approach, because being a poet of process I'm really, alas unavoidably, offering my way of writing, hoping the student will be able to develop his or her own later on.

I have no quarrel with those who reject my way of writing, nor with those who reject the concept of a way of writing. This book is not for all and hardly is intended as the last word. Commenting on a work from the standpoint of the reader, unavoidable at times, can be of enormous benefit, though in my experience it seems to work better with fiction writers than with poets.

Such criticism, offered well, can help young writers develop a method of self-criticism, always a necessity. But at the base of such an approach is the notion that the writer's problems are literary. In truth, the writer's problems are usually psychological, like everyone else's.

I hope this book will be of general interest, and, if you are starting to write poems, that it will help you with your writing. Above all, I hope you'll not take the book more seriously than it is intended. Some of it, though obviously not all, is written in a sense of play. But it is play directed toward helping you with that silly, absurd, maddening, futile, enormously rewarding activity: writing poems. I don't know why we do it. We must be crazy. Welcome, fellow poet.

THE

TRIGGERING

TOWN

Lectures and Essays

on Poetry and Writing

I

Writing
off the Subject

❧

I OFTEN make these remarks to a beginning poetry-writing class.

You'll never be a poet until you realize that everything I say today and this quarter is wrong. It may be right for me, but it is wrong for you. Every moment, I am, without wanting or trying to, telling you to write like me. But I hope you learn to write like you. In a sense, I hope I don't teach you how to write but how to teach yourself how to write. At all times keep your crap detector on. If I say something that helps, good. If what I say is of no help, let it go. Don't start arguments. They are futile and take us away from our purpose. As Yeats noted, your important arguments are with yourself. If you don't agree with me, don't listen. Think about something else.

When you start to write, you carry to the page one of two attitudes, though you may not be aware of it. One is that all music must conform to truth. The other, that all truth must conform to music. If you believe the first, you are making your job very difficult, and you are not only limiting the writing of poems to something done only by the very witty and clever, such as Auden, you are weakening the justification for creative-writing programs. So you can take that attitude if you want, but you are jeopardizing my livelihood as well as your chances of writing a good poem.

If the second attitude is right, then I still have a job. Let's pretend it is right because I need the money. Besides, if you feel truth must conform to music, those of us who find life bewildering and who don't know what things mean, but love the sounds of words enough to fight through draft after draft of a poem, can go on writing—try to stop us.

One mark of a beginner is his impulse to push language around to make it accommodate what he has already conceived to be the truth, or, in some cases, what he has already conceived to be the form. Even Auden, clever enough at times to make music conform to truth, was fond of quoting the woman in the Forster novel who said something like, "How do I know what I think until I see what I've said."

A poem can be said to have two subjects, the initiating or triggering subject, which starts the poem or "causes" the poem to be written, and the real or generated subject, which the poem comes to say or mean, and which is generated or discovered in the poem during the writing. That's not quite right because it suggests that the poet recognizes the real subject. The poet may not be aware of what the real subject is but only have some instinctive feeling that the poem is done.

Young poets find it difficult to free themselves from the initiating subject. The poet puts down the title: "Autumn Rain." He finds two or three good lines about Autumn Rain. Then things start to break down. He cannot find anything more to say about Autumn Rain so he starts making up things, he strains, he goes abstract, he starts telling us the meaning of what he has already said. The mistake he is making, of course, is that he feels obligated to go on talking about Autumn Rain, because that, he feels, is the subject. Well, it isn't the subject. You don't know what the subject is, and the moment you run out of things to say about Autumn Rain start talking about something else. In fact, it's a good idea to talk about something else before you run out of things to say about Autumn Rain.

Don't be afraid to jump ahead. There are a few people who become more interesting the longer they stay on a single subject. But most people are like me, I find. The longer they talk about one subject, the duller they get. Make the subject of the next sentence different from the subject of the sentence you just put down. Depend on rhythm, tonality, and the music of language to hold things together. It is impossible to write meaningless sequences. In a sense the next thing always belongs. In the world of imagination, all things belong. If you take that on faith, you may be foolish, but foolish like a trout.

Never worry about the reader, what the reader can understand. When you are writing, glance over your shoulder, and you'll find there is no reader. Just you and the page. Feel lonely? Good. Assuming you can write clear English sentences, give up all worry about communication. If you want to communicate, use the telephone.

To write a poem you must have a streak of arrogance—not in real life I hope. In real life try to be nice. It will save you a hell of a lot of trouble and give you more time to write. By arrogance I mean that when you are writing you must assume that the next thing you put down belongs not for reasons of logic, good sense, or narrative development, but because you put it there. You, the same person who said that, also said this. The adhesive force is your way of writing, not sensible connection.

The question is: how to get off the subject, I mean the triggering subject. One way is to use words for the sake of their sounds. Later, I'll demonstrate this idea. The initiating subject should trigger the imagination as well as the poem. If it doesn't, it may not be a valid subject but only something you feel you should write a poem about. Never write a poem about anything that ought to have a poem written about it, a wise man once told me. Not bad advice but not quite right. The point is, the triggering subject should not carry with it moral or social obligations to feel or claim you feel certain ways. If you feel pressure to say what you know others want to hear and don't have enough devil in you to surprise them, shut up. But the advice is still well taken. Subjects that ought to have poems have a bad habit of wanting lots of other things at the same time. And you provide those things at the expense of your imagination.

I suspect that the true or valid triggering subject is one in which physical characteristics or details correspond to attitudes the poet has toward the world and himself. For me, a small town that has seen better days often works. Contrary to what reviewers and critics say about my work, I know almost nothing of substance about the places that trigger my poems. Knowing can be a limiting thing. If the population of a town is nineteen but the poem needs the sound seventeen, seventeen is easier to say if you don't know the population. Guessing leaves you more options. Often, a place that starts a poem for me is one I have only glimpsed while passing through. It should make impression enough that I can see things in the town—the water tower, the bank, the last movie announced on the marquee before the theater shut down for good, the closed hotel—long after I've left. Sometimes these are imagined things I find if I go back, but real or imagined, they act as a set of stable knowns that sit outside the poem. They and the town serve as a base of operations for the poem. Sometimes they serve as a stage setting. I would never try to locate a serious poem in a place where physical evidence suggests that the people there find it relatively easy to accept themselves—say the new Hilton.

The poet's relation to the triggering subject should never be as strong as (must be weaker than) his relation to his words. The words should not serve the subject. The subject should serve the words. This may mean violating the facts. For example, if the poem needs the word "black" at some point and the grain elevator is yellow, the grain elevator may have to be black in the poem. You owe reality nothing and the truth about your feelings everything.

Let's take what I think is a lovely little poem, written in 1929 by a fine poet who has been unjustly ignored.

Rattlesnake

> I found him sleepy in the heat
> And dust of a gopher burrow,
> Coiled in loose folds upon silence
> In a pit of the noonday hillside.
> I saw the wedged bulge
> Of the head hard as a fist.
> I remembered his delicate ways:
> The mouth a cat's mouth yawning.

I crushed him deep in dust,
And heard the loud seethe of life
In the dead beads of the tail
Fade, as wind fades
From the wild grain of the hill.*

I find there's much to be learned about writing from this excellent poem. First I think it demonstrates certain truths that hold for much art. The poem grows from an experience, either real or imagined—I only recently found out that this particular experience was real. The starting point is fixed to give the mind an operating base, and the mind expands from there. Often, if the triggering subject is big (love, death, faith) rather than localized and finite, the mind tends to shrink. Sir Alexander Fleming observed some mold, and a few years later we had a cure for gonorrhea. But what if the British government had told him to find a cure for gonorrhea? He might have worried so much he would not have noticed the mold. Think small. If you have a big mind, that will show itself. If you can't think small, try philosophy or social criticism.

The need for the poem to have been written is evident in the poem. This is a strong example of the notion that all good serious poems are born in obsession. Without this poem the experience would have been neither validated nor completed.

The poem has elements of melodrama. All art that has endured has a quality we call schmaltz or corn. Our reaction against the sentimentality embodied in Victorian and post-Victorian writing was so resolute writers came to believe that the further from sentimentality we got, the truer the art. That was a mistake. As Bill Kittredge, my colleague who teaches fiction writing, has pointed out: if you are not *risking* sentimentality, you are not close to your inner self.

The poem is located in a specific place. You don't know where, but you know the poet knows where. Knowing where you are can be a source of creative stability. If you are in Chicago you can go to Rome. If you ain't no place you can't go nowhere.

* From Brewster Ghiselin, *Against the Circle* (New York: Dutton, 1946), p. 60. Reprinted with permission of the author.

The snake is killed gratuitously. The study of modern psychology may have helped some of us become better people. We may treat our children better because we have gained some rudimentary notion of cause and effect in behavior. But in art, as seemingly in life, things happen without cause. They just happen. A poem seldom finds room for explanations, motivations, or reason. What if the poem read

> Because I knew his poison
> Was dangerous to children
> I crushed him deep in dust . . . ?

The poet would be making excuses for himself, and the fierce honesty with which he faces his raw act of murder would be compromised. Nothing in the drama *King Lear* can possibly serve as explanation of the shattering cruelty of Regan and Cornwall when they blind Gloucester. From a writer's standpoint, a good explanation is that Shakespeare knew a lot of creeps walk this earth.

But there's more to be learned from this poem than just artistic principles. They are always suspect anyway, including those I think I find here. Let's move on to the language of the poem.

Generally, in English multisyllabic words have a way of softening the impact of language. With multisyllabic words we can show compassion, tenderness, and tranquillity. With multisyllabic words we become more civilized. In the first four lines of the poem, seven of the twenty-six words, slightly better than one out of four, are two-syllable words. This is a fairly high count unless you are in politics. The snake is sleepy. He presents no threat to the speaker. His dwelling is that of a harmless creature, a gopher. It's almost as if the snake were a derelict, an orphan, a vagabond who sleeps wherever he can. The words "noonday hillside" suggest that the world does not have rigid topography but optional configurations. At 4 P.M. it might not be a hillside at all. We take our identities from our relationships, just as the earth takes its configurations from the time of day, the position of the source of light. This is a warm, fluid world.

With single-syllable words we can show rigidity, honesty, toughness, relentlessness, the world of harm unvarnished. In lines five and six, the snake is seen as a threat, the lines slam home heavy as the fist the poet sees as simile for the head of the snake. But of course, men, not snakes, have fists, and so we might ask: where does the danger really lie here?

The speaker then has a tender memory of the snake in lines seven and eight, and we get two three-syllable words and a long two-syllable word, "yawning." You might note that the poet is receptive to physical similarities of snakes and domestic cats—they look much alike when yawning—just as later he sees and hears the similarity of rattlesnakes to wheat (grain), the way the tail looks like the tassle, the way the rattle sounds like wind in the grain.

In the final five lines the poet kills the snake, faces himself and the moral implications of his act without a flinch or excuse, and we get no multisyllabic words in the entire passage. All single-syllable words, and the gaze is level, the whole being of the speaker honestly laid out, vulnerable on his private moral block. If one acts on the rigid prejudicial attitudes expressed in lines five and six (which the speaker did), and not on the fluid, tender, humane attitudes expressed in the first four lines and lines seven and eight, then in return one is faced with the fully developed, uncompromising picture of what one has done. Forever.

In this poem the triggering subject remains fully in view until late in the poem, whereas the generated object, what the poem is saying, just begins to show at the end but is nonetheless evident. The snake as such is being left behind, and attitudes about life are starting to form. The single-syllable words in the last five lines relentlessly drive home the conviction that all life is related, and that even if life isn't sacred, we might be better off if we acted as if it were. In this case the poet got off the initiating subject late.

I mentioned that one way of getting off the subject, of freeing yourself from memory if you will, is to use words for the sake of sound. Now I must use four lines from an early poem of mine, simply because I can't verify any other poet's process. I know what mine was at the time. These are the first four lines of the fourth stanza of an early poem called "At the Stilli's Mouth."

> With the Stilli this defeated and the sea
> turned slough by close Camano, how can water die
> with drama, in a final rich cascade,
> a suicide, a victim of terrain, a martyr?

When I was a young poet I set an arbitrary rule that when I made a sound I felt was strong, a sound I liked specially, I'd make a similar sound three to eight syllables later. Of course it would often be a slant rhyme. Why three to eight? Don't ask. You have to be silly to write poems at all.

In this case the word "cascade" fell lovingly on my ear and so, soon after, "suicide." I wasn't smart enough to know that I was saying that my need to see things dramatically was both childish and authentic. But "suicide" was right and led to "victim of terrain" and "martyr," associative notions at least, but also words that sound like other words in the passage, "martyr" like "drama" and "water," "victim" like "final" and "Stilli" (Northwest colloquial for Stilliguamish, the river). Instead of "suicide" I might have hit on "masquerade," but that would have been wrong and I hope I would have known it. I might have simply because "masquerade" sounds *too much* like "cascade," calls attention to itself, and to my ear is less interesting. What I'm trying to tell you is that by doing things like this I was able to get off the subject and write the poem. The fact that "suicide" sounds like "cascade" is infinitely more important than what is being said.

It isn't of course, but if you think about it that way for the next twenty-five years you could be in pretty good shape.

2

The Triggering Town

YOU HEAR me make extreme statements like "don't communicate" and "there is no reader." While these statements are meant as said, I presume when I make them that you *can* communicate and can write clear English sentences. ~~cau~~tion against communication because once language exists ~~on~~ly to convey information, it is dying.

Let's take language that exists to communicate—the news story. In a news story the words are there to give you information about the event. Even if the reporter has a byline, anyone might have written the story, and quite often more than one person has by the time it is printed. Once you have the information, the words seem unimportant. Valéry said they dissolve, but that's not quite right. Anyway, he was making a finer distinction, one between poetry and prose that in the reading of English probably no longer applies. That's why I limited our example to news articles. By understanding the words of a news article you seem to deaden them.

In the news article the relation of the words to the subject (triggering subject since there is no other unless you can provide it) is a strong one. The relation of the words to the writer is so weak that for our purposes it isn't worth consideration. Since the majority of your reading has been newspapers, you are used to seeing language function this way. When you write a poem these relations must reverse themselves. That is, the relation of the words to the subject must weaken and the relation of the words to the writer (you) must take on strength.

This is probably the hardest thing about writing poems.

It may be a problem with every poem, at least for a long time. Somehow you must switch your allegiance from the triggering subject to the words. For our purposes I'll use towns as examples. The poem is always in your hometown, but you have a better chance of finding it in another. The reason for that, I believe, is that the stable set of knowns that the poem needs to anchor on is less stable at home than in the town you've just seen for the first time. At home, not only do you know that the movie house wasn't always there, or that the grocer is a newcomer who took over after the former grocer committed suicide, you have complicated emotional responses that defy sorting out. With the strange town, you can assume all knowns are stable, and you owe the details nothing emotionally. However, not just any town will do. Though you've never seen it before, it must be a town you've lived in all your life. You must take emotional possession of the town and so the town must be one that, for personal reasons I can't understand, you feel is your town. In some mysterious way that you need not and probably won't understand, the relationship is based on fragments of information that are fixed—and if you need knowns that the town does not provide, no trivial concerns such as loyalty to truth, a nagging consideration had you stayed home, stand in the way of your introducing them as needed by the poem. It is easy to turn the gas station attendant into a drunk. Back home it would have been difficult because he had a drinking problem.

Once these knowns sit outside the poem, the imagination can take off from them and if necessary can return. You are operating from a base.

That silo, filled with chorus girls and grain

Your hometown often provides so many knowns (grains) that the imagination cannot free itself to seek the unknowns (chorus girls). I just said that line (Reader: don't get smart. I actually *did* just write it down in the first draft of this) because I come from a town that has no silos, no grain, and for that matter precious few chorus girls.

If you have no emotional investment in the town, though you have taken immediate emotional possession of it for the duration of the poem, it may be easier to invest the feeling in the words. Try this for an exercise: take someone you emotionally trust, a friend or a lover, to a town you like the looks of but know little about, and show your companion around the town in the poem. In the line of poetry above, notice the word "that." You are on the scene and you are pointing. You know where you are and that is a source of stability. *"The silo"* would not tell you where you were or where the silo is. Also, you know you can trust the person you are talking to—he or she will indulge your flights—another source of stability and confidence. If you need more you can even imagine that an hour before the poem begins you received some very good news—you have just won a sweepstakes and will get $50,000 a year for the rest of your life—or some very bad, even shattering news—your mother was in charge of a Nazi concentration camp. But do not mention this news in the poem. That will give you a body of emotion behind the poem and will probably cause you to select only certain details to show to your friend. A good friend doesn't mind that you keep chorus girls in a silo. The more stable the base the freer you are to fly from it in the poem.

> That silo, filled with chorus girls and grain
> burned down last night and grew back tall.
> The grain escaped to the river. The girls ran
> crying to the moon. When we knock, the metal
> gives a hollow ring—

O.K. I'm just fooling around. (God, I'm even rhyming.) It looks like the news I got an hour ago was bad, but note the silo replaced itself and we might still fill it again. Note also that now the town has a river and that when I got fancy and put those girls on the moon I got back down to earth in a hurry and knocked on something real. Actually I'm doing all this because I like "l" sounds, "silo" "filled" "girls" "tall" "metal" "hollow," and I like "n" sounds, "grain" "burned" "down" "ran" "moon," "ring," and I like "k" sounds, "back" "knock." Some critic, I think Kenneth Burke, would say I like "k" sounds because my name is Dick.

In this case I imagined the town, but an imagined town

is at least as real as an actual town. If it isn't you may be in the wrong business. Our triggering subjects, like our words, come from obsessions we must submit to, whatever the social cost. It can be hard. It can be worse forty years from now if you feel you could have done it and didn't. It is narcissistic, vain, egotistical, unrealistic, selfish, and hateful to assume emotional ownership of a town or a word. It is also essential.

This gets us to a somewhat tricky area. Please don't take this too seriously, but for purposes of discussion we can consider two kinds of poets, public and private. Let's use as examples Auden and Hopkins. The distinction (not a valid one, I know, but good enough for us right now) doesn't lie in the subject matter. That is, a public poet doesn't necessarily write on public themes and the private poet on private or personal ones. The distinction lies in the relation of the poet to the language. With the public poet the intellectual and emotional contents of the words are the same for the reader as for the writer. With the private poet, and most good poets of the last century or so have been private poets, the words, at least certain key words, mean something to the poet they don't mean to the reader. A sensitive reader perceives this relation of poet to word and in a way that relation—the strange way the poet emotionally possesses his vocabulary—is one of the mysteries and preservative forces of the art. With Hopkins this is evident in words like "dappled," "stippled," and "pied." In Yeats, "gyre." In Auden, no word is more his than yours.

The reason that distinction doesn't hold, of course, is that the majority of words in any poem are public—that is, they mean the same to writer and reader. That some words are the special property of a poet implies how he feels about the world and about himself, and chances are he often fights impulses to sentimentality. A public poet must always be more intelligent than the reader, nimble, skillful enough to stay ahead, to be entertaining so his didacticism doesn't set up resistances. Auden was that intelligent and skillful and he publicly regretted it. Here, in this room, I'm trying to teach you to be private poets because that's what I am and I'm limited to teaching what I know. As a private poet, your job is to be honest and to try not to be too boring. However, if you must choose between being eclectic and various or being repetitious and boring, be repetitious and boring. Most good poets are, if read very long at one sitting.

If you are a private poet, then your vocabulary is limited by your obsessions. It doesn't bother me that the word "stone" appears more than thirty times in my third book, or that "wind" and "gray" appear over and over in my poems to the disdain of some reviewers. If I didn't use them that often I'd be lying about my feelings, and I consider that unforgivable. In fact, most poets write the same poem over and over. Wallace Stevens was honest enough not to try to hide it. Frost's statement that he tried to make every poem as different as possible from the last one is a way of saying that he knew it couldn't be.

So you are after those words you can own and ways of putting them in phrases and lines that are yours by right of obsessive musical deed. You are trying to find and develop a way of writing that will be yours and will, as Stafford puts it, generate things to say. Your triggering subjects are those that ignite your need for words. When you are honest to your feelings, that triggering town chooses you. Your words used your way will generate your meanings. Your obsessions lead you to your vocabulary. Your way of writing locates, even creates, your inner life. The relation of you to your language gains power. The relation of you to the triggering subject weakens.

The imagination is a cynic. By that I mean that it can accommodate the most disparate elements with no regard for relative values. And it does this by assuming all things have equal value, which is a way of saying nothing has any value, which is cynicism.

When you see a painting by Hieronymus Bosch your immediate impression may be that he was a weirdo. A wise man once told me he thought Bosch had been a cynic, and the longer I thought about this the truer it seemed. My gold detector told me that the man had been right. Had Bosch concerned himself with the relative moral or aesthetic values of the various details, we would see more struggle and less composure in the paintings themselves. The details may clash with each other, but they do not clash with Bosch. Bosch concerned himself with executing the painting—he must have—and that freed his imagination, left him unguarded. If the relative values of his details crossed his mind at all while he was painting, he must have been having one hell of a good time.

One way of getting into the world of the imagination is to focus on the play rather than the value of words—if you can manage it you might even ignore the meanings for as long as you can, though that won't be very long. Once, picking up on something that happened when I visited an antique store in Ellettsville, Indiana, I wrote the lines

> The owner leaves her beans to brag about the pewter.
> Miss Liberty is steadfast in an oval frame.

They would have been far harder lines to write had I worried about what's most important: beans, pewter, or liberty. Obviously beans are, but why get hung up on those considerations? It is easier to write and far more rewarding when you can ignore relative values and go with the flow and thrust of the language. That's why Auden said that poets don't take things as seriously as other people. It was easy for me to find that line awhile back because I didn't worry about the relative importance of grain and chorus girls and that made it fun to find them together in that silo.

By now you may be thinking, doesn't this lead finally to amoral and shallow writing? Yes it does, if you are amoral and shallow. I hope it will lead you to yourself and the way you feel. All poets I know, and I know plenty of them, have an unusually strong moral sense, and that is why they can go into the cynical world of the imagination and not feel so threatened that they become impotent. There's fear sometimes involved but also joy, an exhilaration that can't be explained to anyone who has not experienced it. Don't worry about morality. Most people who worry about morality ought to.

Over the years then, if you are a poet, you will, perhaps without being conscious of it, find a way to write—I guess it would be better to say you will always be chasing a way to write. Actually, you never really find it, or writing would be much easier than it is. Since the method you are chasing involves words that have been chosen for you by your obsessions, it may help to use scenes (towns perhaps) that seem to vivify themselves as you remember them but in which you have no real emotional investment other than the one that grows out of the strange way the town appeals to you, the way it haunts you later when you should be thinking about paying your light bill. As a beginner you may only be able to ally your emotions to one thing, either triggering subject or word. I believe it will be easier right now if you stick to the word.

A man named Buzz Green worked with me years ago at the Boeing Company. He had once been a jazz musician and along with a man named Lu Waters had founded a jazz band well known in its day. Buzz once said of Lou McGarrity, a trombone player we both admired, "He can play trombone with any symphony orchestra in the country but when he stands up to take a jazz solo he forgets everything he knows.". So if I seem to talk technique now and then and urge you to learn more, it is not so you will remember it when you write but so you can forget it. Once you have a certain amount of accumulated technique, you can forget it in the act of writing. Those moves that are naturally yours will stay with you and will come forth mysteriously when needed.

Once a spectator said, after Jack Nicklaus had chipped a shot in from a sand trap, "That's pretty lucky." Nicklaus is suppose to have replied, "Right. But I notice the more I practice, the luckier I get." If you write often, perhaps every day, you will stay in shape and will be better able to receive those good poems, which are finally a matter of luck, and get them down. Lucky accidents seldom happen to writers who don't work. You will find that you may rewrite and rewrite a poem and it never seems quite right. Then a much better poem may come rather fast and you wonder why you bothered with all that work on the earlier poem. Actually, the hard work you do on one poem is put in on all poems. The hard work on the first poem is responsible for the sudden ease of the second. If you just sit around waiting for the easy ones, nothing will come. Get to work.

You found the town, now you must start the poem. If the poem turns out good, the town will have become your hometown no matter what name it carries. It will accommodate those intimate hunks of self that could live only in your home-town. But you may have found those hunks of self because the externals of the triggering town you used were free of personal association and were that much easier to use. That silo you never saw until today was yours the day you were born. Finally, after a long time and a lot of writing, you may be able to go back armed to places of real personal significance. Auden was wrong. Poets take some things far more seriously than other people, though he was right to the extent that they are not the same things others would take seriously or often even notice. Those chorus girls and that grain really matter, and it's not the worst thing you can do with your life to live for that day when you can go back home the sure way and find they were there all the time.

3

Assumptions

ASSUMPTIONS lie behind the work of all writers. The writer is unaware of most of them, and many of them are weird. Often the weirder the better. Words love the ridiculous areas of our minds. But silly or solid, assumptions are necessary elements in a successful base of writing operations. It is important that a poet not question his or her assumptions, at least not in the middle of composition. Finish the poem first, then worry, if you have to, about being right or sane.

Whenever I see a town that triggers whatever it is inside me that wants to write a poem, I assume at least one of the following:

The name of the town is significant and must appear in the title.

The inhabitants are natives and have lived there forever. I am the only stranger.

I have lived there all my life and should have left long ago but couldn't.

Although I am playing roles, on the surface I appear normal to the townspeople.

I am an outcast returned. Years ago the police told me to never come back but after all this time I assume that either I'll be forgiven or I will not be recognized.

At best, relationships are marginal. The inhabitants have little relation with each other and none with me.

The town is closely knit, and the community is pleasant. I am not a part of it but I am a happy observer.

A hermit lives on the outskirts in a one-room shack. He eats mostly fried potatoes. He spends hours looking at old faded photos. He has not spoken to anyone in years. Passing children often taunt him with songs and jokes.

Each Sunday, a little after 4 P.M., the sky turns a depressing gray and the air becomes chilly.

I run a hardware store and business is slow.

I run a bar and business is fair and constant.

I work in a warehouse on second shift. I am the only one in town on second shift.

I am the town humorist and people are glad to see me because they know I'll have some good new jokes and will tell them well.

The churches are always empty.

A few people attend church and the sermons are boring.

Everybody but me goes to church and the sermons are inspiring.

On Saturday nights everyone has fun but me. I sit home alone and listen to the radio. I wish I could join the others though I enjoy feeling left out.

All beautiful young girls move away right after high school and never return, or if they return, are rich and disdainful of those who stayed on.

I am on friendly terms with all couples, but because I live alone and have no girlfriend, I am of constant concern to them.

I am an eleven-year-old orphan.

I am eighty-nine and grumpy but with enormous presence and wisdom.

Terrible things once happened here and as a result the town became sad and humane.

The population does not vary.

The population decreases slightly each year.

The graveyard is carefully maintained and the dead are honored one day each year.

The graveyard is ignored and overrun with weeds.

No one dies, makes love, or ages.

No music.

Lots of excellent music coming from far off. People never see or know who is playing.

The farmers' market is alive with shoppers, good vegetables, and fruit. Prices are fixed. Bargaining is punishable by death.

The movie house is run by a kind man who lets children in free when no one is looking.

The movie house has been closed for years.

Once the town was booming but it fell on hard times around 1910.

At least one person is insane. He or she is accepted as part of the community.

The annual picnic is a failure. No one has a good time.

The annual picnic is a huge success but the only fun people have all year.

The grain elevator is silver.

The water tower is gray and the paint is peeling.

The mayor is so beloved and kind elections are no longer held.

The newspaper, a weekly, has an excellent gossip column but little or no news from outside.

No crime.

A series of brutal murders took place years ago. The murderer was never caught and is assumed still living in the town.

Years ago I was wealthy and lived in a New York penthouse. I hired about twenty chorus girls from Las Vegas to move in with me. For a year they played out all of my sexual fantasies. At the end of the year my money was gone. The chorus girls had no interest in me once I was poor and they returned to Las Vegas. I moved here where, destitute in a one-room shack on the edge of town, I am living my life out in shame.

One man is a social misfit. He is thrown out of bars and not allowed in church. He shuffles about the street unable to find work and is subjected to insults and disdainful remarks by beautiful girls. He tries to make friends but can't.

A man takes menial jobs for which he is paid very little. He is grateful for what little work he can find and is always cheerful. In any encounter with others he assumes he is wrong and backs down. His place in the town social structure is assured.

Two whores are kind to everyone but each other.

The only whore in town rejected a proposal of marriage years ago. The man left town and later became wealthy and famous in New York.

Cats are fed by a sympathetic but cranky old woman.

Dogs roam the streets.

The schoolhouse is a huge frame building with only one teacher who is old but never ages. She is a spinster and everyone in town was once in her class.

Until I found it, no outsider had ever seen it.

It is not on any map.

It is on a map but no roads to it are shown.

The next town is many miles away. It is much classier, has a nice new movie house, sparkling drive-ins, and better-looking girls. The locals in my town dream of moving to the next town but never do.

The town doctor is corrupt and incompetent.

The town druggist is an alcoholic.

The town was once supported by mining, commercial fishing, or farming. No one knows what supports it now.

One girl in the town is so ugly she knows she will never marry or have a lover. She lives in fantasies and involves herself in social activities of the church trying to keep alive her hopes which she secretly knows are futile.

Wind blows hard through the town except on Sunday afternoons a little after four when the air becomes still.

The air is still all week except on Sunday afternoons when the wind blows.

Once in a while an unlikely animal wanders into town, a grizzly bear or cougar or wolverine.

People stay married forever. No divorce. Widows and widowers never remarry.

No snow.

Lots of rain.

Birds never stop. They fly over, usually too high to be identified.

The grocer is kind. He gives candy to children. He is a widower and his children live in Paris and never write.

People who hated it and left long ago are wealthy and living in South America.

Wild sexual relationships. A lot of adultery to ward off boredom.

The jail is always empty.

There is one prisoner in jail, always the same prisoner. No one is certain why he is there. He doesn't want to get out. People have forgotten his name.

Young men are filled with hate and often fight.

I am welcome in bars. People are happy to see me and buy me drinks.

As far as one can see, the surrounding country is uninhabited.

The ballpark is poorly maintained and only a few people attend the games.

The ballpark is well kept and the entire town supports the team.

The team is in last place every year.

People sit a lot on their porches.

There is always a body of water, a sea just out of sight beyond the hill or a river running through the town. Outside of town a few miles is a lake that has been the scene of both romance and violence.

AKS

4

Stray Thoughts on Roethke and Teaching

SOME OF this is from memory, twenty-five years of it, and some of it may be wrong. But I'm sure of one thing, on the first day of class in the fall quarter of 1947 he shambled into the classroom, and the awkward, almost self-degrading way he moved made me think he was dressed in "rags and rotting clothes," when actually he was probably in an expensive tailor-made suit. His addiction to bourgeois values, his compulsive need to be loved by all, but most of all the rich, was of course the obverse of the way he felt about himself. In his mind I believe he was always poor and unwashed, and he showed it when he walked.

So I'm certain he wasn't poorly dressed, though I still see him that way. Then I didn't but now I do know he was frightened. "Look," in W. C. Fields-as-gangster voice, "there's too many people in here. If I had my way, I'd have nothing but young chicks, the innocent ones you can teach something." We had to submit poems and he judged. He had to weed. One girl asked if he couldn't be more definite. "You want a quick answer? Get out now." But he laughed. His tenderness toward students often showed through.

He was probably the best poetry-writing teacher ever. That's impossible to prove and silly, but I had to say it just once in print. He was not intellectual in his approach in those days, though I think he changed later. Sometimes he read poems aloud and then couldn't explicate them clearly when he tried. I think he often didn't understand much of what he read. I mean he didn't understand it the way a critic or good literature teacher would understand it. I believe he so loved the music of language that his complicated emotional responses to poems interfered with his attempts to verbalize meaning.

When he read his favorites aloud, Yeats, Hopkins, Auden, Thomas, Kunitz, Bogan, poets with "good ears," something happened that happens all too infrequently in a classroom. If a student wasn't a complete auditory clod, he could feel himself falling in love with the sounds of words. To Roethke, that was the heart and soul of poetry. And that was his strength as a teacher: he gave students a love of the sound of language. His classes were clinics. He performed therapy on the ear.

It was important to some of us in Seattle that he came when he did. It was just great luck. The English Department at the University of Washington in 1947 was in a rut. Vernon Louis Parrington was dead but his influence was not. The approach to literature was Parrington's and little else. Many of the teachers had taken their Ph.D.s right there years before. They had been friends of Parrington, and while many were able teachers, they taught literature as a reflection of historical and sociological patterns of its time. Writers who didn't fit the method were usually ignored—Poe, Henry James.

I lacked anything near an academic imagination, so I just assumed that literature could not be approached any other way. Worse, I simply didn't know who had written what. I'd never heard of Auden, Hopkins, Thomas, or even Yeats. Just the exposure to such poets was worth any tuition fee. But to be exposed to them by a man so passionately committed to their rhythms and tonalities was to be born.

One sad thing about university reputations is that they lag behind the fact. By the time you hear how good an English department is, it is usually too late to go there. But by all accounts Roethke got even better as a teacher as the years went on, though it's hard to imagine his being any better than he was in '47 and '48.

He was a dangerous teacher too. And the danger is a natural one for good poetry-writing teachers who are also good poets. Good poets have obsessive ears. They love certain sounds and not others. So they read aloud what they love, responding to their own obsessive needs in the poetry of others. If he is worth a damn, any poet teaching poetry writing constantly and often without knowing it is saying to the student, "Write the way I do. That's the best sound you can make." The student who shakes this, who goes on to *his* auditory obsessions and who writes the way the teacher never told him, may become a poet. Roethke, through his fierce love of kinds of verbal music, could be overly influential. David Wagoner, who was quite young when he studied under Roethke at Penn State, told me once of the long painful time he had breaking Roethke's hold on him.

For many this hold had enormous psychic proportions because for all his playfulness in poems, it was in poems and poetry that Roethke was playing a profound and dangerous game. Many of Roethke's poems suffer from triviality of spirit for just this reason. When he played and the play didn't unlock the man, only the game remains on the page. Some things are just not meant. But that was the risk he took. A lot of poets don't have the nerve to risk failure.

He was also playful in class, arrogant, hostile, tender, aggressive, receptive—anything that might work to bring the best out of a student. A young man might turn in a poem, read it aloud, and then wait, his heart on the block, and Roethke would say quietly, and ever so slightly sarcastically, "Gee." It was withering. Yet for all of Roethke's capacity for cruelty, it was not a cruel act. Roethke knew that poetry is an art form and a difficult one and that the enthusiasm and hope of the young poet are not enough. You have to work, and you had better get used to facing disappointments and failures, a lifetime of them. Other times he would roar laughter at a funny poem, no matter how inexpertly written. Most students respected his authority not because what he said was intellectually defensible—what an absurd consideration—but because the man was so emotionally honest. Emotional honesty is a rare thing in the academic world or anywhere else for that matter, and nothing is more prized by good students.

He pushed as models the seventeenth-century lyricists—

Herbert, Marvell, Herrick. Whoever he pushed, whatever poem he purred or boomed aloud in class, he was always demonstrating that this, *your* language, is capable of power and beauty. Those of us who had always loved it found out we loved it. Some who hadn't loved it, but had the capacity to, came to love it. The others?

When our poems were coming in void of rhythm he gave demanding exercises, and his finals were evidence of the cruelty in him. I don't have a copy of one of his exams, but here's an exercise I give beginning students once in a while to take home and return in a week or so, and it is very close to what he would give you one hour to do on the final.

Nouns	*Verbs*	*Adjectives*
tamarack	to kiss	blue
throat	to curve	hot
belief	to swing	soft
rock	to ruin	tough
frog	to bite	important
dog	to cut	wavering
slag	to surprise	sharp
eye	to bruise	cool
cloud	to hug	red
mud	to say	leather

Use five nouns, verbs, and adjectives from the above lists and write a poem as follows:

1. Four beats to the line (can vary)
2. Six lines to the stanza
3. Three stanzas
4. At least two internal and one external slant rhyme per stanza (full rhymes acceptable but not encouraged)
5. Maximum of two end stops per stanza
6. Clear English grammatical sentences (no tricks). All sentences must make sense.
7. The poem must be meaningless.

Item 7 is a sadistic innovation of my own.

The point of this exercise will probably be clear to poets.

Too many beginners have the idea that they know what they have to say—now if they can just find the words. Here, you give them the words, some of them anyway, and some technical problems to solve. Many of them will write their best poem of the term. It works, and I've seen it work again and again. While the student is concentrating on the problems of the exercise, the real problems go away for a moment simply because they are ignored, and with the real problems gone the poet is free to say what he never expected and always wanted to say. Euphonics and slant ryhmes are built into the vocabulary of course, and as for item 7, it simply takes the exercise one step further into the world of the imagination. Without it, the exercise is saying: give up what you think you have to say, and you'll find something better. With item 7, it says: say nothing and just make music and you'll find plenty to say. Item 7 is an impossibility of course, but when the student finds out it is, one hopes he will have increased faith in sound and the accidents of the imagination.

Some traditionalists seem to think that forms exist to be solved for their own sake, as if the poet is an engineer. That's just foolish. If a poet finds himself solving the problems of a form simply for the sake of challenge, he has the wrong form. After you've written for a long time, to do it in the forms at all is a little like cheating because you are getting help. But the forms can be important, and when Roethke felt himself going dry he always returned to them. For some students, the exercise will not work because the form is not theirs. They need another or, in some cases, none. Though I can't defend it, I believe that when the poem is coming on with imaginative honesty, there is some correspondence of the form to psychic rhythms in the poet.

The second half of the Roethke final usually consisted of one question, a lulu like, "What should the modern poet do about his ancestors?" "Do you mean his blood ancestors or the poets who preceded him?" I asked. "Just answer the question," Roethke growled.

Roethke could read so effectively that he could set a student's mind rigidly in favor of a poem for years. I came to realize that "The Golden Echo" is not good Hopkins, or even much good for that matter, despite Roethke's fine reading of it. On the other hand, "Easter 1916" still remains a favorite of mine. I think of it as possibly as good a poem as we have in the language, and it was Roethke's reading of it that first prejudiced me.

Just calling attention to what the student is hearing but doesn't know he's hearing can be a revelation. A student may love the sound of Yeats's "Stumbling upon the blood dark track once more" and not know that the single-syllable word with a hard consonant ending is a unit of power in English, and that's one reason "blood dark track" goes off like rifle shots. He's hearing a lot of other things too that I won't go into here. O.K. Simple stuff. Easily observed. But how few people notice it. The young poet is too often paying attention to the big things and can't be bothered with little matters like that. But little matters like that are what make and break poems, and if a teacher can make a poet aware of it, he has given him a generous shove in the only direction. In poetry, the big things tend to take care of themselves.

When I started teaching at the age of forty I was terrified. It was bad enough to hold Roethke up as an ideal and to hope to imitate his methods and techniques rather than my own, but to be told my first day on campus that I was Leslie Fiedler's replacement was a bit too much. I hope I've found my own way of doing things in the classroom, but if I have I didn't find it easily. I found it much easier to shake Roethke's influence as a poet than as a teacher. Only in the last few years have I dropped a phony, blustery way of teaching that was never mine but that I assume was his, though twenty-five years of memory can kink a lot of cable.

Roethke's life would have been easier today in the classroom. Students are far better writers now than we were then. Jim Wright was one of the few students who was writing well in Roethke's classes. I have at least six who are excellent and another dozen good enough to appear in most literary magazines. For one thing, they've had much more exposure to good poems than we ever did. They work hard and have no illusions about writing being easy. I don't think poems come easier for them either, just sooner. They seem to absorb methods of execution faster and to assimilate technique faster than most of us could then.

Mark Strand remarked recently in Montana that American poetry could not help but get better and better, and I'm inclined to agree. I doubt that we'll have the one big figure of the century the way other nations do, Yeats, Valéry. Giants are not the style of the society, though the wind knows there are enough people who want to create them, and not just a few who want to be them. I think we'll end up with a lot of fine poets, each doing his thing. There are a lot of bright and substantial young people writing and a lot of good poetry-writing teachers available to help them, poets who earned the title the hard way and who are generous enough to pass on all that they learned for themselves. Donald Justice and Marvin Bell at Iowa, A. R. Ammons at Cornell, John Logan at Buffalo, David Wagoner at the University of Washington are just a few who come to mind.

Then there's that banal, tiresome question: can writing be taught? Yes it can and no it can't. Ultimately the most important things a poet will learn about writing are from himself in the process. A good teacher can save a young poet years by simply telling him things he need not waste time on, like trying to will originality or trying to share an experience in language or trying to remain true to the facts (but that's the way it really happened). Roethke used to mumble: "Jesus, you don't want to say *that.*" And you didn't but you hadn't yet become ruthless enough to create. You still felt some deep moral obligation to "reality" and "truth," and of course it wasn't moral obligation at all but fear of yourself and your inner life.

Despite Roethke's love of verbal play, he could generate little enthusiasm for what passes as experimentation and should more properly be called fucking around. Real experimentation is involved in every good poem because the poet searches for ways to unlock his imagination through trial and error. Quest for a self is fundamental to poetry. What passes for experimentation is often an elaborate method of avoiding one's feelings at all costs. The process prohibits any chance the poet has to create surrogate feelings, a secondary kind of creativity but in most poems all the poet can settle for. The good poems say: "This is how I feel." With luck that's true, but usually it's not. More often the poem is the way the poet says he feels when he can't find out what his real feelings are. It makes little difference to the reader, since a good poem sounds meant enough to be believed.

"Each newcomer feels obliged to do something else, forgetting that if he himself is somebody he will necessarily do that something else," said Valéry. And Roethke told students to "write like somebody else." There are those usual people who try desperately to appear unusual and there are unusual people who try to appear usual. Most poets I've met are from the latter and much smaller group. William Stafford, at his best as good as we have, is a near-perfect example. It doesn't surprise me at all when the arrogant wild man in class turns in predictable, unimaginative poems and the straight one is doing nutty and promising work. If you are really strange you are always in enemy territory, and your constant concern is survival.

Roethke would probably take issue with that. He had all sorts of odd notions about what makes a poet. Once he told me seriously that we, he and I, being physically large, presented a kind of presence to others, and the pressure we felt from this role dictated by our physical proportions was fundamental to creating poems. He didn't put it that way but that's what he was saying.

Other ideas deserved more serious consideration. Roethke was fond of quoting Rimbaud's idea of the "systematic derangement of the senses," but he always left off the "systematic." When I was in grad school in '49 and '50, the smartest faculty member I knew at the time told me he believed that omission to be important. He felt that Roethke might actually cultivate madness because he believed it essential to writing. That may or may not be true. I suppose it could be argued that all madness is self-created. But what a great compliment to Roethke that people could believe it of him. How many great artists, including Yeats, could be credited with risking their very being for their work? Some poets do burn themselves for their work, like Dylan Thomas, but most prepare themselves for the long haul.

I vaguely recall a class in '48 when Roethke defended madness as important to creativity. I disagree plenty. Madness is crippling anywhere but in art where it belongs and can always find a home. It is obvious that all art is screwy and it is equally obvious that most men who create it are not. They are often "silly like us." Some of them—William Carlos Williams, Wallace Stevens—aren't even particularly silly. What is remarkable is that men handicapped by periods of mental aberration can still fight through and create, while others are simply incapacitated, sometimes forever.

But then we know almost nothing about creativity, where it comes from, what causes it. People who profess to be astounded that Wallace Stevens could be a corporate executive and still write are really saying, "How could he be a poet when he's not like me?" There are a lot of poets who aren't like you, even if you're a poet.

Most creative-writing teachers in Roethke's day worth mentioning were formalists, and formality was an end in itself. Obligation to play "by the rules" remained paramount. As a teacher Roethke stood virtually alone at the time. For Roethke the rules were simply one way to help a poet get to the gold. Certain areas he wisely left alone. I think he instinctively knew that fool's gold is what fools end up with, and a teacher can do nothing about that.

In one area Roethke lacked sophistication at moments. He was far too competitive for his own good, and while I'm far more competitive than I admit, I believe that it is only in periods when you can transcend your competitive instincts that you can write. A sound analogy could be made with hitting a baseball. If you concentrate on beating a particular pitcher, your chances of hitting him are not as good as they are if you can ignore him until he disappears and you can concentrate on the ball. And your chances of writing a poem are greatly reduced if you are trying to beat Robert Lowell or T. S. Eliot or anybody else. Roethke's love of prizes, rave reviews, and applause would sometimes prevent him from emphasizing to the student the real reward of writing—that special private way you feel about your poems, the way you feel when you are finishing a poem you like.

Yet he knew it, and in rare moments it showed. Once he said to me, that nervous undergrad who wanted the love of the world to roar out every time he put a word down, "Don't worry about publishing. That's not important." He might have added, only the act of writing is. It's flattering to be told you are better than someone else, but victories like that do not endure. What endures are your feelings about your work. You wouldn't trade your poems for anybody's. To do that you would also have to trade your life for his, which means living a whole new complex of pain and joy. One of those per lifetime is enough.

5

Nuts and Bolts

THAT'S WHAT these are. Nuts and bolts. My nuts and bolts. For me they helped, or once helped, and some still do. I'm stating them as rules, but of course they are no more than suggestions— I find the axiomatic tone preferable to a lot of qualifiers. If these work for you, good.

Use number 2 pencils. Get a good pencil sharpener and sharpen about twenty pencils. When one is dull, grab another.

Don't write with a pen. Ink tends to give the impression the words shouldn't be changed.

Pen or pencil, write with what gives you the most sensual satisfaction. When I said use number 2 pencils, I was really saying that when I use number 2 pencils I feel good putting words on paper.

Write in a hard-covered notebook with green lined pages. Green is easy on the eyes. Blank white paper seems to challenge you to create the world before you start writing. It may be true that you, the modern poet, must make the world as you go, but why be reminded of it before you even have one word on the page? The lines tend to want words. Blank paper begs to be left alone. The best notebooks I've found are National 43–581.

Don't erase. Cross out rapidly and violently, never with slow consideration if you can help it.

When young it's normal to fear losing a good line or phrase and never finding anything comparable again. Carry a small pocket-size notebook and jot down lines and phrases as they occur. This may or may not help you write good poems, but it can help reduce your anxiety.

Make your first line interesting and immediate. Start, as some smarty once said, in the middle of things. When the poem starts, things should already have happened. (Note: White unlined paper gives you the feeling nothing has happened.) If Yeats had begun "Leda and the Swan" with Zeus spotting Leda and getting an erection, Yeats would have been writing a report.

When rewriting, write the entire poem again. If something has gone wrong deep in the poem, you may have taken a wrong turn earlier. The next time through the poem you may spot the wrong path you took. If you take another, when you reach the source of your dissatisfaction it may no longer be there. To change what's there is difficult because it is boring. To find the right other is exciting.

If you want to change what's there, use the same words and play with the syntax:

> This blue lake still has resolve.
> This lake still blue with resolve

By playing with the syntax we've dropped a weak verb and left the sentence open with a chance for a stronger one. But maybe you can't find a stronger verb, or you still want to end the sentence:

> This lake's still blue with resolve.

You may object that the meaning has changed, that you are no longer saying what you want to say. Never *want* to say anything so strongly that you give up the option of finding something better. If you *have* to say it, you will.

Sometimes the wrong word isn't the one you think it is but another close by. If annoyed with something in the poem, look to either side of it and see if that isn't where the trouble is. You can seldom be certain of the source of your annoyance, only that you are annoyed. Sometimes you may feel dissatisfied without justification. The poem may be as good as it will get. Often a word is not right but very close: dog—hog, gill—gull, hen—hun.

When you feel a poem is finished, print it. The time needed to print a word is a hair longer than the time needed to write it. In that extra moment, you may make some lovely changes. Had Auden printed his poems he might not have needed the happy accident of the typist inadvertently typing "ports" for "poets," a mistake that helped a poem considerably.

Read your poem aloud many times. If you don't enjoy it every time, something may be wrong.

Put a typed copy on the wall and read it now and then. Often you know something is wrong but out of fear or laziness you try to ignore it, to delude yourself that the poem is done. If the poem is on the wall where you and possibly others can see it, you may feel pressure to work on it some more.

Use "love" only as a transitive verb for at least fifteen years.

End more than half your lines and more than two-thirds your sentences on words of one syllable.

Don't use the same subject in two consecutive sentences.

Don't overuse the verb "to be." (I do this myself.) It may force what would have been the active verb into the participle and weaken it.

> Once out of nature I shall never be taking
> My bodily form from any natural thing,

> But such a form as Grecian goldsmiths are making
> Of hammered gold and gold enameling . . .

If you ask a question, don't answer it, or answer a question not asked, or defer.

> What stunned the dirt into noise?
> Ask the mole, he knows.

If you can answer the question, to ask it is to waste time.

Maximum sentence length: seventeen words. Minimum: one.

No semicolons. Semicolons indicate relationships that only idiots need defined by punctuation. Besides, they are ugly.

Make sure each sentence is at least four words longer or shorter than the one before it.

Use any noun that is yours, even if it has only local use. "Salal" is the name of a bush that grows wild in the Pacific Northwest. It is often not found in dictionaries, but I've known that word long as I can remember. I had to check with the University of Washington Botany Department on the spelling when I first used it in a poem. It is a word, and it is *my* word. That's arrogant, isn't it? But necessary. Don't be afraid to take emotional possession of words. If you don't love a few words enough to own them, you will have to be very clever to write a good poem.

Beware certain words that seem necessitated by grammar to make things clear but dilute the drama of the statement. These are words of temporality, causality, and opposition, and often indicate a momentary lack of faith in the imagination.

Temporality: *meanwhile, while, as* (at the same time as), *during, and* (implying "and at the same time")

> But no one comes
> and the girl disappears behind folding doors
> while the bus grinds and lurches away.

No one comes.
The girl disappears behind folding doors.
The bus grinds and lurches away.

Here, the words "and" and "while" point up a relation that can be provided by the mind. "While" simply means that two things happen at the same time. Without "while" they happen at the same time. What was funny about "Meanwhile, back at the ranch" was the superimposition of the words on the screen over a shot of the ranch. We are told what was being demonstrated. It would be boring if not maddening to live in a world where all things were labeled. Where "house" would be stamped on a house.

In my skull
death echoes the song of the wind as it
hands up each winter defeat.

In my skull
death echoes the song of the wind. The wind
hands up each winter defeat.

I'm not saying eliminate these words from your vocabulary. I'm saying don't use them out of grammarphobia to make connections clear. Note in the above example the relative values of the two statements were eliminated by removing the "as." With the "as" the temporal relation of the two statements was stated, and the mind gave or wanted to give more value to one than the other. Now they are equal. Style and substance may represent a class system. The imagination is a democracy.
Causality: *so* (as a result), *because, thus, causing*

So I wait here, high outside the city, while in
your reality dreams come only at will.

I wait here, high outside the city.
In your reality, dreams come only at will.

Don't put signposts to relationships.
Opposition: *yet, but*

My hard bed waits for me
yet that room is cold now.

My hard bed waits for me.
That room is cold.

We knew that prairie would stay empty
but horses filled the dawn.

We knew that prairie would stay empty.
Horses filled the dawn.

Often the opposition is far more dramatic if you don't call attention to it. Sometimes, the opposition isn't opposition.

The sun rises slowly like an old man,
Fish rise in shadows
but elude me like virtues.

The sun rises slowly like an old man.
Fish rise in shadows.
They elude me like virtues.

All these trails we can follow,
the tails of comets that disappear at sunrise
but stay on the dark tablet of the eyes for months.

All these trails we can follow,
the tails of comets that disappear at sunrise
stay on the dark tablet of the eyes for months.

The poem need not end on a dramatic note, but often the dramatic can be at the end with good effect.

All these trails we can follow,
the tails of comets that disappear at sunrise
stay for months on the dark tablet of the eyes.

Beware using "so" and "such" for emphasis. They're often phony words, uttered. "He is so handsome." "That was such a good dinner." If "so" is used, it is better to have a consequence.

> Our cows have eaten grass turned brown so long
> *and* wind *just* barely *lifts and* stirs the leaves.

> Our cows have eaten grass turned brown so long
> the cows turned brown. Wind barely stirs the leaves.

This leads us to more complicated problems, so let's shift into a higher gear. More happened in the revision than I expected. By obeying one silly "rule," I found myself forced to cut the fat from the statement that followed. That is the advantage of making up rules. If they are working, they should lead you to better writing. If they don't, you've made up the wrong rules. Almost all young poets are using more syllables than necessary, more words than needed. In the above example, by using four additional words to avoid the phony sound of "so," a word used for emphasis that begs our reaction in some way that I find annoyingly undignified, I found four unnecessary words in the next line—"and," "just," "lifts," "and"—and took them out to make the statement fit this line. Here, I'll rewrite a first stanza to make it adhere logically, then offer the stanza as written by the student, then suggest other versions.

> In St. Ignatius the swallows hit
> the dead end of the sky
> then turn on themselves. They fly over Indians
> who thanked the church long ago
> and changed into trees, and over the boys
> who are tired of fishing and throw a dog off the bridge.

Here, the swallows remain to account for the Indians and the boys, as if Indians and boys had no right in the poem without some relationship with the swallows. Here, the stanza as submitted:

> In St. Ignatius the swallows hit
> the dead end of the sky

> then turn on themselves. Indians
> thanked the church long ago
> and changed into trees. Boys are tired
> of fishing and throw a dog off the bridge.

Much better. Once something is established it is left, not used
to make sure the next thing belongs.* A few problems left.
Too many "the"s. Now if we take out the first one we risk
sibilance by having the *s* of "Ignatius" run into the *s* of "swallows." Maybe a comma will do.

> In St. Ignatius, swallows hit
> the dead end of the sky
> then turn on themselves.

In the next two lines the words "long ago" seem somewhat flat
because they follow what is dramatically important. Let's try

> Long ago
> Indians thanked the church
> and changed into trees.

The next two lines seem too leisurely for the pace of the poem
to me. A possibility:

> Tired of fishing
> boys throw a dog off the bridge.

Putting it together:

> In St. Ignatius, swallows hit
> the dead end of sky

* The reader may object that here I'm limiting the young poet's chance of
writing a good poem early, and that is true. Letting the birds hold things
together is perfectly good technique. But to prepare a young writer for the
long haul, I believe it is better to emphasize style (his or her way of writing) as the binding force and to promote faith in the imagination. If it
means making more problems for the moment, it may result in fewer later
on. Creating artificial problems early can help the poet through major
problems later. No need to worry it will ever get *too* easy. Plenty of problems will remain.

> then turn on themselves. Long ago
> Indians thanked the church
> and changed into trees. Tired of fishing
> boys throw a dog off the bridge.

But three lines in a row we've withheld the subject a moment. Too much stylistic monotony? Let's pop the subject home first at least once:

> Swallows hit
> the dead end of sky in St. Ignatius
> then turn on themselves. Long ago
> Indians thanked the church
> and changed into trees. Tired of fishing
> boys throw a dog off the bridge.

Note that the monotony of self-introspective life in St. Ignatius is implied by the approximately equal length of the sentences (word count fourteen, ten, ten, syllabic count eighteen, fourteen, twelve) and the relatively flat tone. Connections are not stated, yet we know the three statements are connected. They are connected because the same poet wrote all three. That is, they are products of one vision that, along with style, becomes the adhesive force. This adhesive force will be your way of writing. Assume the next thing belongs because you put it there. The real reason may be clearer later.

Whatever the merits of the stanza (the inevitability of the progression remains in doubt, a risk normal to the flat tone), at least it moves from one thing to another without excuses and for no reasons external to the poem, such as narrative logic, or description. When writing assume the right of all things to be resides in the things themselves.

But that can get you in trouble too.

Check Your Barometer

> Feeling alone, they reach for stars,
> Making sure they have ten sides.
> Higher, puffs of cotton hang motionless,
> Suspended.

> Mist fills the air and drops of water
> Too heavy to stay aloft make targets on a mirror.
> Men from the tower will never believe.
> They are protected.
> Dead, grey with what might be age, the tree
> Becomes encased in flame
> Heat.
> Trails of perspiration race down the furs
> It will be gone soon
> That will give the snow a chance to melt.

Flat-toned as the St. Ignatius stanza is, we had a sense of someone behind it. In this poem, the world seems separated from
the poet's capacity to respond to it. What is missing is a stance.
Since I believe any stance, no matter how melodramatic, is
preferable to none, I'll rewrite the poem and take liberties to
simulate some inner landscape that, if not now missing alto-
gether, is at least negligible.

> They hate me, the men who reach for stars
> and save for export those with ten sides.
> Outside my window, puffs of phony cotton
> on the cottonwood hang high as stars
> and I can't reach them. Mist dots my mirror
> mornings, and my face stays vague.
> Men in the tower, between the big dipper and dew,
> with disdain look down where I wave.
>
> Grey with age, with fatigue, some day the cottonwood's
> bound to explode in flame, the sweat
> that runs the bark will be my sweat,
> some old shame perspiring again, the hurt.
> The cotton will drift down warm to my hand.
> The snow will run.

Not much better, but certainly, in all its corn, more human.
Perhaps, in some ways the first poem seems just as good, but
did anyone write it? At least a fool wrote the second version.

Formal verse can help the young poet locate things to say
but can also obligate him to say things he wouldn't say except

to fill out the form. Here is a far better than average try by a
young man just starting.

From Eola, Illinois, in the Summer

1.

My brother left today before the storm.
His Buick raised the dust along the road,
then he was gone. He left behind the farm,
and, in the place we once had talked, there showed
the weathered white of planks our barn turned old.
The roads are paved for miles beyond our town,
where the women sit the afternoons alone.
And somewhere east Chicago grates across the ground.

2.

Our cows have eaten grass turned brown so long
and wind just barely lifts and stirs the leaves.
We've lost our dogs. Our summertimes are wrong,
our town grown old with heat. And no one gives.
At home, in stores, our men complain of sleeves—
their sleeves too warm, too long for August days.
But then, we like our town and all its ways.
We never went so wrong they had to build a bar.

3.

The afternoon he went away we sat
outside the house to eat and talk out loud.
We said that Illinois was always flat,
so goddamned flat it wanted to be plowed.
We hate the mountains. We would rather crowd
or sprawl across the plains. Our farms are dead.
But while we talked the clouds rolled in like lead,
so hot and dark we finally moved inside to talk.

4.

That something hard about the storms out here—
we watched it move among the farms to ours
and felt it shake the tree. We heard it near
the gate, then rain began to pelt the cars

and slosh the yard and spatter down the flowers.
For once, at least, the streets could look that bare
without excuse—but who would ever care?
We have our houses still, my friend, and they are white.

5.
So nothing came, and nothing went, it seems.
We all had talked about the chance of hail,
tornados, floods. But now we know they're dreams,
and all that ever really comes is mail.
And sitting on the porch, it's just as well.
But sometimes thoughts about those raging storms
that crack the peaks creep up and touch our arms.
We hate our lives. We hate our farms.

Obviously there's much padding, but there's also more honesty
than usual for an early poem. Two problems strike me as important. The form is often forcing the poet to make the line
unit a unit of grammar as well as of sound. This could easily
be remedied. For example:

> The afternoon he went away we sat
> outside the house to eat and talk. We believed out loud
> that Illinois [etc.]

The poet said "talk out loud" because he wanted to make the
rhyme, and the easiest way to make it is to make the unit of
sound also the unit of sense. Consequently he is over-end-
stopping, padding, and being redundant. The form is forcing
him to excesses of words.

The other problem is a failure to realize that rhymes are
often effective if they come at unexpected moments. Let's go
to work on the last stanza.

> Nothing came. And nothing went. It seems
> we talked and talked about the chance of hail,
> tornados, flood. Now we know they're dreams.
> All that ever comes is mail.
> It's just as well.

> Sitting on the porch we dream those storms
> that crack the peaks and tingle in our veins.
> We hate our lives. We hate our farms.

That isn't right either. But we are getting there. A sudden shortening of the line from the established pattern can make a rhyme more interesting. (I don't know why he numbered the stanzas. I forgot to ask him.) Of course, there's much more work to be done.

A few possibilities. Since he's padding, the form may be too big. He might try a seven-line stanza, rather than an eight. Given that English is deficient in good full rhymes, he might consider using slant rhymes to give himself more chances. Too many of his rhyme words are words that can be used only as one part of speech. Others could be used more than one way. "Farm" and "storm" can also be verbs, for example, but by limiting them to nouns he increases the possibility he will write end-stops. For all the faults of the poem, the effort is commendable. The impulse to write seems strong and immediate, and he should learn much working this way.

Let's take one more complete poem because it demonstrates several important problems.

Cycle

> Old, one of the first to know; he senses
> but does not care.
> There are no fathers and sons, only old bucks,
> and young ones,
> He is tough, strong, in his prime at five, or
> six.
> Ready!
> He tests the air in impatience, his nose impassioned
> from the burning smell.
> Real memory is beyond him, but lying somewhere
> in the unmeasured distance is instinct.
> Testicles pulsing with life, becoming strong
> after the long dormancy of winter, flood his
> body with hormones of desire.

> Restless, he urinates, paws and stamps, his
> range smelling to high heaven.
> She is ready, close to estrus.
> She came easier than the others,
> His defense still smooth and shiny
> Madness, heat, fondness nearly between them.

This is a good example of a poem that does not move. It contains more information than is necessary. The poet is milking every last detail out of the situation. He is depending on the drama of the event, the mating of deer, to carry the poem. The suspense lies outside the poem, and by referring to that suspense, the situation itself, the poet hopes to build suspense in the poem with rhetorical devices: "testicles pulsing with life," "Restless, he urinates, paws and stamps," "She is ready, close to estrus." The Swan is fooling around and Leda is getting ready.

The first seven lines are description, characterization, and scene-setting. When the poem says "Ready!" it really is asking if we are ready for the poem to begin. The poem is starting way too early.

The poem cannot be written because the poet reduced the possibilities by sticking with one established subject. He wanted one subject to carry the poem and felt that everything must refer to what prompted the poem. Here are some things the poet could have done to avoid trying to wring every last drop of drama out of a single event. He could have located the event. Where did it happen? Was there a river nearby? If not, does the poem need one? If so, put it there. A wheatfield? A mountain? What if the deer mated in an abandoned mining town? That would give the poem many more things to work with. For example, the following words would be available: sluice, flume, gold, silver, ore, slag, lead, graves, miners, church, photos, gun, rifle, grub, shaft. Certainly with words like those available the poet need not have been forced by the limitations he put on himself to use "impassioned," "unmeasured distance," "instinct," "life," "dormancy," "hormones of desire." If he had located the poem, he might have found a vocabulary that could make the poem dramatic in itself. What if the deer mated on the streets of Butte? How do deer mate in Burma? The poet might have expanded the possibilities, even if he had to fictionalize the situation to do it. He could have introduced elements that are alien to the subject yet could be part of the scene: rattlesnake, bison, wheat, avalanche. How about elements that could not be part of the scene but could be part of the poem: submarine, pyromaniac, tyrant, crocodile, gangster, saint, begonia—but, you may be saying, how could *they* be part of the poem? That may be the wrong question. Asked seriously and often it could lead you back to those frustrated hormones of desire.

The examples used are either made up or taken from poems submitted in my classes at the University of Montana. My thanks to the students for permission to use their work.

6

In Defense of Creative-Writing Classes

I BELIEVE worthwhile things can't be justified. I would never try to justify sex, fishing, baseball, or Mozart. My grandfather used to say that some whiskey is better than others, but there is no bad whiskey. That might well apply to sex and Mozart. They seem to be in a class of their own.

Creative-writing classes seem better put in a class with fishing and baseball. I've had bad fishing, I've seen and played bad baseball, and I've seen and taught bad creative-writing classes.

Let's put one matter aside. I'm not getting into some semantic rhubarb about the term "creative writing." Call it "imaginary writing" or whatever you want. It is called "creative writing" in most places, and you know what I'm talking about.

It's not new. For around 400 years it was a requirement of every student's education. In the English-speaking world, the curriculum for grammar and high school students included the writing of "verses." In the nineteenth century, when literary education weakened or was dropped from elementary and secondary education, colleges picked it up, all but the creative writing. Creative writing was missing for 100 years or so, but in the past 40 years it has returned.

It was never really missing, just missing from educational institutions. Writing is hard and writers need help. Pound was a creative-writing teacher for Eliot, Williams, Hemingway, and Yeats. Yeats, by Pound's admission, was Pound's creative-writing teacher in return. Nothing odd about that. If we creative-writing teachers are doing our job, we are learning from the students. If we are writers as well as teachers, we are also stealing from them, and they from us. As long as people write, there will be creative-writing teachers. It's nice to be on the payroll again after a century or more of going unemployed.

So, if any defense is needed, it is the defense of creative writing in school, specifically, if we are speaking of college, in the English department, where creative writing seems to find itself. Creative writing belongs in the university for the same reason other subjects do: because people will pay to study them. If you challenge the right of creative writing to be in the university, to be fair you'd have to challenge a long list of other subjects in the catalogue. (Not a bad idea, but let's not wreck the economy beyond repair.)

The English department seemed a logical place for creative writing, perhaps because it was already involved with other writing, critical and expository. It can be argued that all writing is creative writing, since if one is writing the way one should, one does not know what will be on the page until it is there. Discovery remains the ideal. Another reason for putting creative writing under English is the assumption that reading and writing are closely related. It is even assumed that reading naturally precedes writing, though common sense tells us that in the beginning that could not have been the case.

From experience and observation, I've come to believe reading has as serious a relation to writing as do any number of activities such as staring pensively out the window or driving to Laramie. A very serious relation at times. At other times no relation at all. The writing of a poem or story is a creative act, and by "creative" I mean it contains and feeds off its own impulse. It is difficult and speculative to relate that impulse to any one thing other than itself. Please understand, I'm speaking of the impulse to write and not the finished work.

Sometimes I talk about the triggering subject, about locating a home for the impulse to the poem. I'm trying to let students know that like Baudelaire's albatross, our chances of flying off to the beautiful selves we always were increase if we start out with our talons on deck, even if we must endure the teasing and ridicule of those coarse Philistine sailors. I'm convinced that a genuine impulse to write is so deep and volatile it needs no triggering device other than the one it already has. When not writing, a writer may search for a triggering device, and literature is one of several places to find it. But the urge to search came from need, and that remains mysterious, evidently complete in itself.

So here we are, in the English department, in some ways privileged, in others the victims of bigotry surprisingly unsubtle, coming from educated colleagues.

And we are privileged. Let me cite some evidence. For about 100 years we weren't here and no one seemed to miss us. I'll clear some of the air right now by admitting I believe in the traditional teaching of literature and I believe that the teaching of literature is the most important function of an English department. I don't know if the present Ph.D. system is the best way to prepare teachers of literature. It seems to have worked well in many cases, and I'm not imaginative enough to dream serious alternatives. One thing it does not do is teach people to write. When I read some academic writing I marvel that as common and everyday as language is, it would have the effrontery to get in the way of all that thinking. I've seen sentences that defy comprehension written by people with doctorates in English from our best universities. So have you. And I doubt that academic writing will improve until academics believe Valéry, who said he couldn't think of anything worse than being right. In much academic writing, clarity runs a poor second to invulnerability.

One of our privileges as creative writers is that we are vulnerable people who hold jobs in an environment where self-protection is a way of life. Our vulnerability can be enjoyable, perhaps even enviable. In some ways it is phony. I confess I'm not nearly as naïve as I sometimes appear, and the innocence feigned by some creative writers approaches being offensive. Our vulnerability can also be unhealthy, the social counterpart of the kind of exposure some report to the police.

Not only does the Ph.D. system graduate many people

whose writing approaches the disgraceful, there is contempt for good writing among some scholars. When I was in graduate school it was common to hear a published scholar who wrote clearly referred to as a popularizer.

Scholars seem to assume that if you can read you can write. It's sad to see someone with a fresh Ph.D. coast for a few years, understandably after such a grueling period of work, then embark on a book. It is a struggle because the scholar doesn't realize one simple thing about writing: it is like shooting a basketball. You've got to stay in shape and practice to do it well. It is not a natural reward of study, and having an education does not mean you can write well whenever you want.

We creative writers are privileged because we can write declarative sentences, and we can write declarative sentences because we are less interested in being irrefutably right than we are in the dignity of language itself. I find words beautiful that ring with psychic truth and sound meant. If such a choice were possible, I would far rather mean what I say than say what I mean. To use language well requires self-sacrifice, even giving up pet ideas. George Garrett had no small point when he proposed that all literature teachers be made to take a course in creative writing: "they might at least learn a measure of common humility."

We are privileged because we are supported by those who are threatened by our cavalier intellectuality. Scholars look for final truths they will never find. Creative writers concern themselves with possibilities that are always there to the receptive.

And we are privileged in other ways. The rewards of our teaching are relatively immediate and tangible. I often find ex-students published in literary magazines. At Iowa where I visited for a year, Mike Ryan and Maura Stanton, who both later won the Yale Series of Younger Poets contest, were in my class—though I'm sure they learned little from me *that* year. James Welch, Dave McElroy, and Rick DeMarinis have been in my classes at Montana. If I'm corrupt enough to give myself some undeserved credit, it is because pride blinds. I would guess that around forty of my ex-students are now publishing. Many creative-writing teachers can list far more than I can.

Compare that with the lot of the academic professor. I mean a fine academic professor, a whiz in class, one who brings an energy to teaching born out of love of the material, whose stimulating lectures ignite in students more than they knew they could know. Unless that professor is lucky enough to be in one of a dozen or so schools, he has at best a general sense of what has happened in the minds of his students. The tangible evidence is slight. Years from now one may take a Ph.D. somewhere and write a fine critical book. One. Maybe two. In a lifetime of giving much, the good academic professor will finally realize little in return.

Side note: Teachers, like policemen, firemen, and service personnel, should be able to retire after twenty years with full pension. Our risks may be different, but they are real. In twenty years most teachers have given their best.

I'm not sure the sudden popularity of creative-writing courses is a privilege. It may be our ruination. It is becoming a sore point in English departments. The enrollment in creative writing increases and the enrollment in literature courses is going down. I'm not sure why and I'm not sure the trend is healthy.

There's more than a little truth in the explanations offered by some academic professors. They cite the increasing narcissism of students, the egocentric disregard of knowledge, the laziness, the easy good grades to be had in the writing courses. And in creative writing, especially undergraduate classes, we get more than our share of ego trippers who don't want to write any more than they want to read. Certainly in most of our academically exclusive schools we find creative writing missing or offered as a grudging gesture. And in those schools as well as in many of our large state universities, creative writers suffer a status something like Japanese prisoners in World War II.

As for grades, if anyone will tell me how to grade creative writing, I'll be grateful. The only people who seem to feel creative writing should be graded are administrators far removed from the firing line. Many creative-writing teachers give high grades for a very good reason. If you write you know how difficult it is. A lot of people teaching freshman composition can't write much better than the students and have no idea how hard good writing is. Another reason for high grades in creative writing is that most teachers of creative writing disdain grades and are trying to tell others what they should realize themselves—grades don't mean a thing. When a student asks me for a grade I try to let him know I don't care what his grade is and he shouldn't either. I'll give you an *A* if you promise to feel cheap. But that's naïve, I fear, trying to improve human nature.

Other reasons may account for the dwindling popularity of lit courses and the increased demand for creative writing. Some lie in the way the mind reacts to different forms of knowledge. For example, here are two pieces of knowledge, one literary, the other biological.

1. In John Dryden's "An Essay on Dramatic Poesy," toward the end of his long discourse, Neander says to Crites, "As for your instance of Ben Jonson, who, you say, writ exactly without the help of rhyme; you are to remember 'tis only an aid to a luxuriant fancy, which his was not: as he did not want imagination, so none ever said he had much to spare. Neither was verse then refined so much to be an help to that age, as it is to ours. Thus then the second thoughts being usually the best, as receiving the maturest digestion from judgment, and the last and most mature product of those thoughts being artful and laboured verse, it may well be inferred, that verse is a great help to a luxuriant fancy; and this is what that argument which you opposed was to evince."

2. All groupers are born females and later become males.

Which offers the most interesting possibilities? For the scholar? For the critic? For a poet? For a stand-up comedian? When you read the two pieces above, some of you may have become poets for a moment. A few may have become comedians. If you were still a scholar or a critic, you may have had some regrets. If you felt excited about the imagistic and metaphorical possibilities suggested by the odd biological history of groupers, you might head for a creative-writing course. When universities were smaller and more exclusive, you were either ignored or forced to adjust. You studied Dryden, and, if you weren't interested, feigned interest or you got out. Today the department budget in most state universities is based on enrollment statistics. A department may not get more budget line positions if the enrollment goes up, but it might very well lose them when enrollment goes down. The professional administrator is everywhere, and English departments are not above using statistics swelled by people who find that with some subjects the difference between knowing and not knowing is simply too small to bother about. It is better than going under to accommodate people for whom knowing is less fun at times than guessing.

It hardly endears creative writing to the average academic that he has spent years of hard work getting the Ph.D. degree, involving himself deeply in scholarship and criticism, and now his position depends on the presence of people who don't care about his expertise. It may get worse. A lot of creative writers, students and teachers, don't help the situation. They don't give the academic, who often has much to offer them, a chance. There is hostility, and in some universities it is bad.

Happily, Montana has very little hostility between creative writers and academics. An occasional nasty remark, usually disguised and sometimes intended as a joke, and some rather bizarre treatment of graduate creative-writing students by a couple of isolated academics is about as far as it has gone. That is not the case everywhere. But we have a tradition of creative writing that goes back many years. Walter van Tilburg Clark taught creative writing for years at Montana. My first creative-writing teacher at the University of Washington, Grant Redford, a fine teacher with a wretched class, came from the University of Montana. Faculty and students, creative writers have enjoyed full status here.

At the risk of sounding self-righteous, I've found that in schools where such hostility runs deep, it usually originates with the academics. The old explanations are easy to hop on: the professor of literature always dreamed of being a poet, academics are jealous of the psychic energy of writers, aca-

demics feel that creative writers don't work hard enough.
Whatever there is to these explanations, I find them wanting.
I've come to believe that the hostility between academics and
creative writers is simply the result of small-mindedness on
both parts. It is failure to recognize and grant each other's
worth. It is a xenophobia not worthy of people who call themselves educated.

I started teaching at the age of forty. In the fourteen years
I've been at it I've talked to many students and faculty, and
I've reluctantly come to a few conclusions. It hurts to state
why I believe students are turning away from literature courses
because even at fifty-four maturity is not my strong point, and
polemic tends to make me either nervous or bored and with-
drawn. I do not like a fight, and I hope what I say doesn't start
one.

A young recent Ph.D. asked me to attend his class to dis-
cuss some of my poems with his students. I like the young
man and was pleased he wanted to teach my work. It was a
good class. The teacher had done his work well. That was
obvious from the enthusiastic attention the students brought
to the work being discussed and the intelligent way they made
points.

One student asked how I'd come to write "The Lady in
Kicking Horse Reservoir," one of the poems they were study-
ing. My answer was straightforward. I'd had a love affair. The
woman dumped me for someone else. I was brokenhearted
and vengeful, but cowardly. So in real life I suffered but in
the poem I had my revenge—at least early in the poem.

A few days after the class, the teacher told me he had been
very surprised at my answer, that he didn't know poets used
life that way. I was surprised at his surprise and asked him
where he'd assumed poems came from. He replied that he'd
believed a writer sits alone in a room and makes things up.

Understand this is a bright young man. A good teacher.
He has a Ph.D. in literature from one of our very best universities. Where did he get such ideas about writers? The
answer is obvious. He got them from the same place he got his
education.

One of my reluctant conclusions is that the Ph.D. system

tends to train people to teach literature as if it is some grand, mysterious system that has little or nothing to do with human existence. Obviously enough good teachers come out of the system to justify it. But I fear such a system attracts its fair share of people who are eager to put knowledge between themselves and their lives. To put it bluntly, dull people. As the punch line of the old joke goes, "I've been going through my notes and it turns out I *have* read *Hamlet*."

I've even heard academics refer to popular teachers as "entertainers." To have interest in literature and to communicate that interest is of secondary value at best. True integrity is often willfully equated with dullness. That's not a recent development, either. If anything, it was worse when I was a student.

Another reason for declining student interest in literature courses is a tendency of academic professors to establish and maintain emotional advantages over the students. They seem to have acquired knowledge in order to feel superior to those without it. A strange attitude for a teacher—not wanting to give and share. They're not as good at this as business executives are. Maybe that's why they must limit their victims to the young. One rule for all who want the advantage over others: never show your feelings. The capacity to hide feelings is the one trait I found common to all high-level corporation executives during my thirteen years in industry. Of course, it helps if you don't have any feelings to hide.

This tendency to hold the advantage over the student is not a new development, either. It too was worse when I was in school. But then it was considered normal, and it did not turn students away from the literature courses. Students were less sophisticated and assumed that superior knowledge gave license for behaving as if one had superior social status. A lot of students today would rather not learn Milton than be made to feel inferior because they didn't already know his work.

That makes academics sound petty. But damn it, some of them are petty. In one large university the senior faculty voted against publishing the graduate catalogue because they objected to their names' appearing with names of junior faculty members. It's a wonder what so-called educated people will do to look important. It's no wonder that a lot of young people don't want to study under them.

If I had to limit myself to one criticism of academics it would be this: they distrust their responses. They feel that if a response can't be defended intellectually, it lacks validity. One literature professor I know was asked as he left a movie theater if he had liked the movie, and he replied, "I'm going to have to go home and think about it." What he was going to think about is not whether he liked the movie, but whether he could defend his response to it. If he decided he couldn't, presumably he'd hide his feelings or lie about them.

Academics like these, and fortunately they are far from all the academics, give students the impression that there's nothing in literature that could be of meaningful personal interest. If I seem to be sniping, forgive me. There are great academics and I'm proud to know some of them, glad that I can work in the same profession with them. If my criticism seems harsh, please know I still consider academic professors indispensable to an English department. Whatever the curses of creative writing, it is still a luxury. If there's a choice between dropping Shakespeare studies or advanced poetry writing, I would not defend retention of the writing course. It is not as important to the education of the students.

Whatever my criticisms of some academics, I'm old enough to know that education as a way of improving the self remains a fluffy ideal. Academics have no corner on human failure. We creative-writing teachers have at least our fair share, and speaking personally, I'm in no position to be critical of the weaknesses of others. We must live with some things. There may not be enough good people to go around, and most people aren't very good at what they do. The excellent teacher may be as rare as the excellent automobile mechanic. The Ph.D. system may not attract enough good people, but the M.F.A. system in creative writing has some shortcomings too.

One glaring weakness of the system is that it places in teaching positions people who have not demonstrated that their impulse to write is real and lasting. It is simply too easy to pass oneself off as a writer in a university. I'm in favor of all M.F.A. graduates remaining out of school for at least ten years before they are considered for a teaching position. This is a cruel proposal, given the economic pressure to build a a career. For it to work humanely, schools should be willing to count that ten years as time on the job and to hire the writer at the associate professor level, but without tenure until the writer demonstrated his ability to teach creative writing. This way, one will have already published and presumably would continue. The writing is there to be judged, published or not, and the writer has demonstrated a durable impulse to write. One would hold or lose the job on the basis of one's ability to teach. Creative-writing instructors often write and publish because that is their role and they must do it to hold their job. Once they receive tenure, they stop writing. We are perpetuating ourselves and the system.

Some may hop on this idea and say: yes, and then the writer would be forced to subject himself or herself to outside experience. Experience outside the university is just what the writer needs. But I am doubtful. I believe the writer creates experience as needed to satisfy impulses to write. The odd and not so odd are everywhere, and landscapes never stop. For a writer it is a matter of receiving, responding, converting, and appropriating. A writer will do that anywhere.

The graduate writing program has some serious problems. One is how we judge students for acceptance to the program. I think Yeats was right when he observed that what comes easy for the bad poet comes with great difficulty for the good. We accept those who, in our opinion, seem to be the best writers. But we may be accepting those who have absorbed technique rapidly because no obsessions normal to the good writer were there to get in the way. In forty years a celebrated poet may turn out to be someone who was rejected by graduate writing programs. I see no way around this. We have to go on the samples of writing submitted. The strength of the impulse behind a piece of writing is a hard thing to judge, and we are wise not to try. Most young writers haven't learned to submit to their obsessions.

We can't ignore the overwhelming evidence in favor of creative-writing classes. Names like Tennessee Williams, Arthur Miller, Kurt Vonnegut, Flannery O'Connor, Robert Lowell,

Theodore Roethke, on and on, testify in one way or another to the validity of writing classes. But let's load the dice and say all the good writers would have done it anyway. Maybe they would have. If I am that fatalistic about writing, how can I justify creative-writing classes? A dozen years or so back I was asked that in front of a huge audience, and my answer is still the same: I don't. I just take the money. This time let me dignify the question with some other equally serious answers.

A good creative-writing teacher can save a good writer a lot of time. Writing is tough, and many wrong paths can be taken. If we are doing our job, creative-writing teachers are performing a necessary negative function. And if we are good teachers, we should be teaching the writer ways of doing that for himself all his writing life. We teach how not to write and we teach writers to teach themselves how not to write. When we teach how to write, the student had best be on guard.

What about the student who is not good? Who will never write much? It is possible for a good teacher to get from that student one poem or one story that far exceeds whatever hopes the student had. It may be of no importance to the world of high culture, but it may be very important to the student. It is a small thing, but it is also small and wrong to forget or ignore lives that can use a single microscopic moment of personal triumph. Just once the kid with bad eyes hit a home run in an obscure sandlot game. You may ridicule the affectionate way he takes that day through a life drab enough to need it, but please stay the hell away from me.

The best argument for a creative-writing class is one I learned long ago, in 1940 in high school. I didn't know I'd learned it until years later, but I'm slow picking up the important lessons. West Seattle High School was fairly middle-class. A few children of Japanese truck farmers and some of us from Youngstown and White Center helped preserve what I snobbishly prefer to think of as peasant vitality. Belle McKensie, the creative-writing teacher, had fiery red hair and shapely legs the boys remarked on outside of class, and she had loud concepts of democracy and equality that she practiced when her temper didn't interfere. One student, named Hughes (I think), had moved to West Seattle from Oklahoma. One had to be unusually ingratiating and aggressive to find friends among the little snobs who banded together at West Seattle High. I suppose that's standard for a high school. Hughes was shy, a stranger, just one of many of the 2,000 students passing through, unnoticed, lonely, and probably miserable.

One day he read aloud a theme he had written—we had to read our work aloud to get credit. It was a true story about an evening some older boys had taken him to a whorehouse. He had been fourteen at the time, and he was candid about his fears, his attempts to appear courageous and confident to the older boys, his eventual panic and running away. We were a bit apprehensive when he finished. That story could have gotten him thrown out of most classes in the school. McKensie broke the silence with applause. She raved approval, and we realized we had just heard a special moment in a person's life, offered in honesty and generosity, and we better damn well appreciate it. It may have been the most important lesson I ever learned, maybe the most important lesson one can teach. You are someone and you have a right to your life. Too simple? Already covered by the Constitution? Try to find someone who teaches it. Try to find a student who knows it so well he or she doesn't need it confirmed.

In the thirty-eight years since that day in McKensie's class, I've seen the world tell us with wars and real estate developments and bad politics and odd court decisions that our lives don't matter. That may be because we are too many. Architecture and application form, modern life says that with so many of us we can best survive by ignoring identity and acting as if individual differences do not exist. Maybe the narcissism academics condemn in creative writers is but a last reaching for a kind of personal survival. Anyway, as a sound psychoanalyst once remarked to me dryly, narcissism is difficult to avoid. When we are told in dozens of insidious ways that our lives don't matter, we may be forced to insist, often far too loudly, that they do. A creative-writing class may be one of the last places you can go where your life still matters. Your life matters, all right. It is all you've got for sure, and without it you are dead. These days, the joke is even less funny.

If a lot of people were not already willing to run from

their lives, the demand for creative-writing classes would be greater. Disappearing into the hugeness of system is not unattractive. I know. I've attended large universities and worked in giant corporations, and I've found anonymity to be wondrously seductive. Something pulls some of us back from that tempting disappearance. Call it the obsessive and irresistible love of being alive, if you can stand the rhetoric. It is born of the certainty we will disappear fast enough. Oblivion needs no help from us. Long ago, in the first poem in his first book, James Wright told himself and us

> Be glad of the green wall
> You climbed across one day,
> When winter stung with ice
> That vacant paradise.

It is paradise *because* it is vacant, like a blank sheet of paper. It is paradise because the vacancy is there for us to fill momentarily, and we are here to fill it. No matter how justified our despair, we still live in a world where circumstances that make death preferable to life are limited by our revulsion. When moments that support our awareness of ourselves and each other, fond or sad, immediate or mnemonic, insist, some of us would not deny them any more than we would deny our lives. That anyone or anything says they are not important is vivid proof that they are. Creative-writing classes give us a chance to be glad of the green wall.

7

Statements of Faith

❧

BEHIND several theories of what happens to a poet during the writing of a poem—Eliot's escape from personality, Keats's idea of informing and filling another body, Yeats's notion of the mask, Auden's concept of the poet becoming someone else for the duration of the poem, Valéry's idea of a self superior to the self—lies the implied assumption that the self as given is inadequate and will not do.

How you feel about yourself is probably the most important feeling you have. It colors all other feelings, and if you are a poet, it colors your writing. It may account for your writing.

Mr. Auden believed that the fear of failure is the nemesis of American writers. We are so competitive, he says, that we want to destroy all other writers, want to write the one book that is so great it will eliminate all competition forever. Since the imagination cannot cope with such a task, the result is creative impotency. That, he says, is why so many American writers write one book of considerable promise and then nothing else.

Auden may have found this idea reinforced by his relations with Roethke. If you were beating Roethke in a game of 21 in basketball, he would complain throughout the game that he had thrown his right shoulder out years before and it had never come back. You didn't have to be Jerry West to beat Roethke at 21, but his implication was clear. Were his shoulder all right, you, or Jerry West, wouldn't stand a chance. He'd wipe you out, Buster.

Despite Roethke's unconvincing and often endearing machismo, as a poet he found that failure haunted him far less than success. The possibility that the poem might fail some inner ideal may have been haunting, but acclaim from the outside demanded terrifying adjustments.

Many American poets seem to feel personally worthless unless they write. One can easily imagine that, given the conditions of the mind, the feelings of worthlessness may become indistinguishable from the impulse to write.

When people tell a young poet he is good, they may be doing him some disservice. They are telling him he is not worthless and so unwittingly they are undercutting what to him seems his need to write. I'm not suggesting we run about telling young poets how awful they are to ensure they keep on writing. They will tell themselves that often enough without our help.

I've known of cases where the poet's behavior was adversely affected by "success," that is, acclaim. Yes, I really am great and everything I put down is great so I don't have to work hard anymore. Yes, I am great and so have license for whatever I do to others. No, I am not great. I am unworthy of this praise and once others see how outrageous I really am they'll disdain me and I can get back to writing. I am great and will be a part of literature. Therefore, I must constantly grow through style changes to ensure my worth as an artist of stature.

It would be ideal if some instrument could be developed that could measure a writer's capacity for success and then just enough acclaim, money, and praise could be doled out to keep the writer going.

Two classic American short stories: Hemingway's "Soldier's Home" and Faulkner's "Barn Burning." In Hemingway's story, the protagonist, Krebs, by birth and circumstance is an insider. As a result of his experiences in a war and his own sensitivity, he feels alienated and outside. In Faulkner's story, the protagonist, Snopes, a little boy, by birth and circumstance is an outsider who wants desperately to be in. He wants to be a part of what, from his disadvantageous position, seems a desirable life. His father is criminally insane and in his own mind can justify anything he does. Snopes is torn between loyalty to his father and the urge to protect "decent" people from his father's viciousness. In the end, he informs on his father and as a result his father is killed while committing a crime.

Not from birth and circumstance, but by virtue of how they feel about themselves and their relation with the world, as revealed in their poems, many American poets see themselves as (or really are) Krebs or Snopes.

Krebs: William Carlos Williams, Ezra Pound, Richard Wilbur, e. e. cummings, Wallace Stevens, Allen Ginsberg.

Snopes: T. S. Eliot, Theodore Roethke, Robert Lowell, William Stafford, Louise Bogan, James Wright, Galway Kinnell, A. R. Ammons.

Of the two, the Snopes poets would probably have a harder time handling success, since the Krebs poets could be successful without feeling they had violated their heritage. The Snopes poets would feel that their heritage has some deep emotional claim to their loyalties. The Krebs poets could write their best poems without fingering their fathers. The Krebs poets would feel that if something is wrong with their relations with the world, the fault is not entirely theirs.

Both would find success hard to adjust to. For a Krebs poet success means accepting values he knows are phony. For a Snopes poet, success could mean he has cast aside all people (including himself) he believes are doomed to failure and whom he continues to love. In both cases the result could be self-hatred and creative impotency.

Certain feelings can lead to certain stances in the poem. If the feelings are strong enough the stances may be over-stances, or poses. This might result from extreme feelings of shame and degradation (Roethke) or intense self-hatred (Dylan Thomas). Such poets I find specially rewarding because they risk looking silly in their posturings. That may be why they appeal to the rest of us.

The mind, no matter how antisocial it seems, attaches outrageous importance to things others consider unimportant or dull. Poets of overstance admit this. When I read Eliot's definition of the objective correlative, I sometimes have the urge to add at the end the words "in polite society."

To feel that you are a wrong thing in a right world should lead a poet to be highly self-critical in the act of writing. Just as you must assume everything you put down belongs because you put it there (just to get it down at all) you must also assume that because you put it there it is wrong and must be examined. Not a healthy process, I suppose! But isn't it better to use your inability to accept yourself to creative advantage? Feelings of worthlessness can give birth to the toughest and most welcome critic within.

Poets who fail (and by fail I mean fail themselves and never write a poem as good as they know they are capable of) are often poets who fail to accept feelings of personal worthlessness. They lack the self-criticism necessary to perfect the poem. They resist the role of a wrong thing in a right world and proclaim themselves the right thing in a wrong world (not the same thing as Krebs if that's what you are thinking—Krebs doesn't care much for the world or himself). In a sense they are not honest and lack the impulse (or fight it) to revise and perfect.

I feel so strongly about these matters that I am superstitious. I don't know how many young people I've heard (usually men) proclaim themselves great artists and then fade into the woodwork. I believe that the moment you declare yourself great you put a curse on yourself. You can get away with it in baseball (Johnny Bench) or boxing (Muhammed Ali) if you have the physical gifts to back it up. But the poet who says "I am the greatest" has damned himself forever.

Jealousy is impossible for a poet because he has written every poem he loves. Among the beautiful poems I've written are "Leda and the Swan," "Memories of West Street and Lepke," "The Farm on the Great Plains," "A Guide to Dungeness Spit," and perhaps a hundred more.

When I meet a poet who is jealous of the *poems* of others (reputation is another matter), I'm sure that poet has not yet written a poem as good as he knows he can. When you have done your best, it doesn't matter how good it is. That is for others to say.

If your life must be validated in all its anger and hostility to a world you don't want (Krebs), or in all its regret and loneliness in a world that doesn't want you (Snopes), the validation waits inside you to find itself in words on the most ordinary sheet of paper.

There are as many ways of feeling about oneself as there are people. What I am talking about is not limited to poets. In others it is often far more sad and far more seriously damaging.

However a poet feels about himself, he feels it in such a way that at moments he can play with the feeling.

I once believed Mallarmé's statement that within him was that which would count the buttons on the hangman's vest was a claim to cold-blooded objectivity. Now I believe it was acceptance of a world where the trivial and definite can vie for attention with the emotionally overwhelming.

Is Mallarmé's notion so much different from the man who, after surviving a terrible auto crash and with his wife lying bloody in the car, steps out and begins to pick up small bits of glass? Are words bits of glass? Buttons on a hangman's vest? On a lover's clothes?

Should you reject yourself because you count buttons and pick up glass when all civilization tells you: please, this is hardly the time?

An act of imagination is an act of self-acceptance.

One reason many poets drink so much may be that they dread the possibility of a self they can no longer reject. Alcohol keeps alive a self deserving of rejection. If the self as given threatens to become acceptable, as it often does after years of writing, it must be resisted, or the possibility that the poet will not write again becomes a monstrous threat.

When Faulkner, replying to the question, "Why do you drink so much?" answered, "For the pain," he may not have meant to cure the pain. He may have meant to keep it alive.

Writing is a way of saying you and the world have a chance. All art is failure.

A long time back, maybe twenty-five years ago, a reviewer (*Hudson Review*, I think) ridiculed William Carlos Williams for saying one reason a poet wrote was to become a better person. I was fresh out of graduate school, maybe still there, filled with the New Criticism, and I easily sided with the reviewer. But now I see Williams was right. I don't think Williams was advocating writing as therapy, nor the naïve idea that after writing a poem one is any less depraved. I believe Williams discovered that a lifetime of writing was a slow, accumulative way of accepting one's life as valid. What a silly thing we do. We sweat through poem after poem to realize what dumb animals know by instinct and reveal in their behavior: my life is all I've got. We are well off to know it ourselves, even if our method of learning it is painfully convoluted.

When you write you are momentarily telling the world and yourself that neither of you need any reason to be but the one you had all along.

I believe the reason Roethke sought out the wealthy for companionship during his last years was that he had come close to accepting a self he had once spitefully rejected. But he couldn't believe it and wanted proof that the self he was starting to accept was truly of worth. In his mind, only the right and "well chosen" could verify this.

I believe the political conservatism of many poets in this culture is a personal conservatism mistakenly appropriated to politics, where it least belongs. If you are a wrong thing in a right world, then you should change and the world should remain the same. More important is the imagination's impulse to create unknowns out of knowns (my thanks to Madeline De-Frees for this idea). If the knowns keep changing, the process of creating the unknowns is constantly threatened because the base of operations is unstable. It is natural though not necessarily healthy for poets to prefer a world left alone to remain just as it is forever.

A Snopes poet obviously finds conservatism natural. If Snopes grew up to be a political radical (an understandable development and perhaps a laudatory one), it's doubtful he would be a poet. Though it is possible he would call himself one.

One problem for modern poets is the wholesale changes in what we see—the tearing down of buildings, the development of new housing, the accelerated rate of loss of all things that can serve as visual checkpoints and sources of stability. There is more than just temporal correlation between the destruction of the Louis Sullivan buildings in Chicago and the Sharon Tate murders in Los Angeles.

With the accumulated losses of knowns, the imagination is faced with the problem of preserving the world through internalization, then keeping that world rigidly fixed long enough to create the unknowns in the poem. (Rilke spoke of this.) Today, memory must become thought's ally. Though the process becomes more complicated and challenging, I believe the accelerated loss of knowns accounts for the increasing number of people writing poems.

The self as given is inadequate and will not do. I remember I was distrustful of both Eliot and Roethke when late in their careers they announced they were happy. But they were being honest. Every poem a poet writes is a slight advance of self and a slight modification of the mask, the one you want to be. Poem after poem the self grows more worthy of the mask, the mask comes closer to fitting the face. After enough poems, you are nearly the one you want to be, and the one you want to be closely resembles you. The happiness Eliot and Roethke spoke of is one that cannot be observed by others because it is only a different way one has come to feel about oneself. "Nearly" and "closely," not "exactly" and "perfectly." Hope hard to fall always short of success.

8

Ci Vediamo

❧

I'LL TELL you some stories. I won't press the point, but I hope these stories demonstrate some of the problems involved in writing. Problems of how memory and the imagination modify and transform experience, problems of stances you might have to take or drop to order language into a poem. Some of that heavy stuff.

In World War II I was a bombardier based in Italy. I was on the American side, but let me assure you the history books are right. We won. If you had seen me bomb, you might have doubts.

I was the world's worst. One day I missed not only the target in the Brenner Pass, but the entire Brenner Pass itself, thirteen miles wide at that point. My fear made hard concentration difficult and I didn't trust the equipment. I would glance over the bombsight as we approached the target, having made the siting and adjustments, and think: That doesn't look right. The sight must be crazy.

In 1963 I went back. It was not easy. I was almost forty. My wife and I quit good jobs in Seattle and went to Italy to live for a year on savings. Once our savings were gone we would be broke and jobless. That worried me. I'd never had much confidence in my ability to find a job. If it hadn't been for my wife's courageous resolve, I could not have made the break. I tried for a grant—a Guggenheim, I think—but no luck.

Some friends urged us to go. Some people I worked with at the aircraft factory found it hard to understand what I was doing. One colleague asked me seriously why I was going to a land with all that violence. What violence? Imagine living in the United States and thinking Italy violent.

I really didn't know why I was going. When people asked, the only answer I could find was: I just want to see it again.

I came to one Italy in 1944 and another in 1963. The 1963 Italy was filled with sparkling fountains, shiny little cars that honked and darted through well-kept streets, energetic young men and beautiful, well-dressed young women, huge neon signs that said CIT and COMPARI and CINZANO in bright blue or red or green.

The 1944 Italy I remembered brown and gray and lifeless. Every city, every small town reeked. No young men in the towns and no cattle in the fields. The war had taken the men and the Germans had taken the cattle. That was the Italy I expected to find when I came back. I hate to admit it, but that was the Italy I wanted to find. I fell in love with a sad land, and I wanted it sad one more time.

I must confess to a perverse side of self. I give and give to beggars, but there is in me something that feeds on the now of things. Of course I want it all better, want poverty gone forever from the world. But I also have the urge to say, "Stay destitute three more days, just until I finish my poem." I'm ashamed of that in me.

There were good reasons for loving the sad early Italy, the best being that Italy was earth. The sky became more and more frightening as I neared my thirty-fifth bombing mission. If I made thirty-five I would go home. In the air I could disappear forever in one flash, fall to my death when my chute failed to open, or fall in my open chute to a German mob that would beat me to death as they had others. In the sky there seemed as many quick ways to die as there were thermals and flak bursts jolting the plane. I could age on earth, die slowly enough to make some final, corny speech—I'm a going, partner—the way they did in the old movies. On earth, you can say good-bye.

My first memory of Italy is a stone wall, about three feet high, grape vines, and a soft evening sky, a blue I'd not seen before. The wall and vines were close to the tent where our

bomber crew spent one night on the outskirts of a town called
Goia. I never saw Goia again. The next day we flew to the base
where we would live for the next eight months. It took us
eight months to fly thirty-five missions because the winter
turned bad in 1944, and we lost a month of good flying weather
in the fall when our squadron was assigned to fly gasoline to
a British Spitfire base in Lyon.

The closest town of any size was Cerignola, eleven miles
away. I still can't say it very well. I find it hard to make the
"gn" sound in Italian. This was the province Puglia (Apulia),
on the Adriatic side, perhaps forty miles inland below the spur.

I found out later that Cerignola had a bad reputation in
Italy. Some Italians considered it an unfriendly if not dangerous town. American G.I.s were to be off the streets by five in the
afternoon. There were rumors of stabbings and robberies. I
doubt they were true. If anything, we were the hostile ones,
bitter at finding ourselves stuck in that lonely, austere land,
caught up in a war we had nothing to do with starting. Since
we never saw the enemy as we passed five miles above him
on the bomb run, we imagined the Italians were enemies. Of
course, until late in 1943 they had been, though often not very
willing ones. If you are frightened and resentful, it's easier if
you have a defined enemy. On bad days, the Italians were our
enemies.

The closest large city was Foggia, about thirty miles west.
To get there, you had to go through Cerignola. I used to hitchhike to Foggia and sit in the Red Cross alone, drinking coffee,
eating cookies, and listening to records. I played two over and
over on the little player, Benny Goodman's "Don't Be That
Way," and Tommy Dorsey's "Song of India." I often hitchhiked those thirty miles just to hear Lawrence Brown's trombone passage on the Goodman, or Bunny Berrigan's trumpet
solo on the Dorsey. After hearing the records many times, I
would hitchhike back to the base across the drab, flat countryside.

The British had bases in the area, and I was fascinated by
the British. One day in Foggia, I found a little hotel bar. The
only other people there were the bartender and three English
soldiers. "I say," one of them said in an accent I found deli-

cious, "will you ever forget your feelings when it was announced that Hitler had attacked Russia?" "Oh, I say. Wasn't
that the grossest miscalculation," another answered. "Yes," the
third said, "if it hadn't been for that, we would have been
for it." I've never forgotten that exchange. They seemed
worldly to me, their view wide and deep.

Hitchhiking back from Foggia one day, I was given a ride
in a British command car. I saw the colonel in the back seat
lean forward and tell the driver to stop. The colonel was so
poised, polite, and charming that I asked him if he was a
member of the aristocracy, and he said he was. He was an earl.
He asked me many questions about our missions, and I told
him everything he wanted to know. I didn't care that it was
classified information. Enough close flak bursts had convinced
me the Germans knew our altitude. Besides, I am loose-tongued
by nature. Had I been captured, long before the Gestapo
brought those blowtorches and pliers to my cell, I would have
been known as Blabbermouth Hugo.

The colonel reminded me very much of the actor Herbert
Marshall. I envied his composure, his gentility, and easy good
manners. Although in no way did he register amazement or dis-
approval, I imagined he found it strange that a nervous, over-
talkative, boorish boy could be an American officer. I had the
impression he found me interesting but decided that was
simply his aristocratic training—always let the serfs know you
have a keen interest in their lives. I hoped that some day I'd
perfect my own composure and detachment. I wanted very
much to be like the earl, or Herbert Marshall.

Bob Mills, a pleasant, civilized young man, had attended
Stanford University for a year or two. A bombardier, he had
grown a long, handsome black moustache, and his warm,
fluid personality got him elected president of the squadron
officers' club. He was given $500 in *lire* and the task of buying
more liquor for the club. He was also assigned a jeep, and he
asked me to go along with him to Barletta on the Adriatic
coast where the liquor was produced and sold.

Among other dangers our imaginations had created was
the danger of bandits, and we took our .45 automatics. I had

my gun (piece, if you're still G.I.) stuffed in my right trench-coat pocket, and I felt a bit like Humphrey Bogart sitting there in the jeep as the olive trees and grass and magpies passed by. Mills drove, the huge wad of *lire* tucked away on him somewhere. It was a good way to break the boredom, bouncing through the Italian countryside.

Though, like most G.I.'s, I couldn't hit a cow with a .45 if I was holding her teat, the bulge and weight of the gun in my pocket gave me a sense of security. It is one thing to kneel, helpless, in the nose of a bomber jolted by bursts of flak fired five miles away by men whose names you will never know and whose faces you will never see. You trust to luck. You are not about to master your fate.

But this was the earth and the gun was real. The bandits who came pouring out of those hills would be real and I would shoot them. I and Bob Mills and Humphrey Bogart in our trenchcoats. We would blast them with our .45s and they couldn't help but see our faces set in resolve, our glittering eyes.

We rolled into Barletta in about two hours, maybe less. The children picked us up and ran after us, filling the day with sisters for sale and pleas for cigarettes and candy. There must have been thirty already by the time we stopped at the distillery (perhaps not the right word), and more were running toward us. And great good soldier that I was, when I stepped out of the jeep my gun fell from my pocket and crashed to the stone street. I bent down to pick it up, and when I stood up the street was empty. Not a sound. Not a child anywhere. I stood in the eerie emptiness of that silent street and did not then comprehend what fear the war had put in those children. I wondered why they weren't fascinated by the gun as, I was sure, American children would have been.

You'll notice that the men I wanted to be are strong men, men in control. Humphrey Bogart. Herbert Marshall. Each in his own way tough. My urge to be someone adequate didn't change after the war. When I gave up fiction as a bad job and settled back into poems for good, I seemed to use the poems to create some adequate self. A sissy in life, I would be tough in the poem. An example:

Index

The sun is caked on vertical tan stone
where eagles blink and sweat above
the night begun already in the town.
The river's startling forks, the gong
that drives the evening through the pass
remind the saint who rings the local chime
he will be olive sometime like a slave.

Screams implied by eyes of winded eagles
and wind are searing future in the stone.
The cliff peels off in years of preaching water
and the cliff remains. The saint is red
to know how many teeth are in the foam,
the latent fame of either river bed
where trout are betting that the saint is brown.

Flakes of eagle eggshells bomb the chapel
and the village ears of sanctuary dumb.
In a steaming room, behind a stack
of sandbagged books, the saint retreats
where idols catch a fever from his frown.
The saint is counting clicks of eagle love.
The river jumps to nail a meaty wren.

And April girls enlarge through layers
of snow water, twitching fish and weeds
and memories of afternoons with gills.
If a real saint says that he could never
see a fiend, tell that saint to be here,
throat in hand, any Friday noon—
delirious eagles breed to tease the river.*

    I don't even understand that one anymore. Once I did, though, or I wouldn't have published it. (I have a smattering of integrity, thank you.) Note how definite the voice is. How

* From *Death of the Kapowsin Tavern* (New York: Harcourt, Brace & World, 1965), p. 21. Reprinted with permission of author.

strong the command to the self tries to be. How the poem urges the man in it to accept reality in all its cruelty and diffuseness. And I even took a private pride in the difficulty of the poem. I wasn't afraid of anything. No, sir. You don't understand my poems? Screw off, Jack. But in real life, be my friend. Like me. Like me.

I went to Cerignola far more often than to Foggia. It was smaller but closer. All restaurants were off-limits in Italy during the war, and there were few places to go in Cerignola. The Red Cross, of course, but they didn't have swing records. When I went to Cerignola, I usually got drunk in a little makeshift bar. The girl who waited tables was short, stocky, and stacked. The love-starved G.I.s watched her as she brought the *spumante* to the tables. They taught her to whip her hand along her hip as if she were a cowboy making a fast draw. Every time she did it, pointed her finger at us and depressed her thumb hammer, the soldiers howled.

The bar had a band, trumpet, accordion, and drums. The trumpeter's best number was "Stardust," and he played it often while the G.I.s rolled their eyes and exclaimed. I sat alone and drank *spumante*, listened to the music, watched the girl's ripe behind bulge her dress, and wondered what the raucous enlisted men would think if they knew how self-conscious I was. Not because I was the only officer there, but because I was too timid to approach a woman and feared a lifetime of sexual deprivation. I laughed when I knew it was expected and made a point now and then of the attraction I felt for the girl. I could not have had her even if she had consented, but I wanted her and I could let the world know that.

My first time in the Cerignola area had been from August 1944 through March 1945. It was April when I saw it again, April 1964. The countryside was green with grain and the weather pleasantly warm. Cerignola seemed bigger. A nice-looking hotel operated next to the building that had been the local Red Cross. A door or two from the hotel was where the bar had been, with the finger-pistol-packing *mamma mia* waitress. I wasn't sure now which door it was. Shops open for business. People of all ages were in the streets. No children begged us for cigarettes or candy or offered their sisters for sale. The streets seemed unusually wide, and I noticed iron grillwork on balconies of recent apartment buildings.

Foreigners seldom visit Cerignola, and we were curiosities. I got into a discussion with some young men and suddenly realized we were circled by at least a hundred onlookers. "Who," I shouted involuntarily in English, "are all these people?" and they moved off slowly as if they understood from the volume of my voice that I didn't want my every word a public matter. A comic-looking old man stared at my wife, his lower lip quivering as if he were about to break into tears of resentment. In a tobacco shop, a man went into rapture when he found I could speak Italian, wretched as my Italian is, all 300 words of it. Everywhere we walked, people trailed us. The owner of a delicatessen said he remembered me. I was the soldier who got into a fight with another soldier over a dog. No, I wasn't.

I wanted to find two places. One was the squadron area where we had lived for eight months, and the group head-quarters nearby. The other was a field somewhere south of a town called Spinazzola. What kind of a field? Just a field, with tall grass, slanted uphill from the road. An empty field.

To go anywhere on our own in Italy during the war, we hitchhiked. What a discouraging time, standing beside a dirt road as truck after truck went by, empty, the drivers staring past us down the road. Some drivers laughed as they passed. They were bitter, resentful at finding themselves in this drab land with little to break the boredom but some awful Italian booze. They expressed their frustration by refusing us rides. Some even slowed down, and we would run to the truck only to have it pull away from us. That was the driver's idea of fun. And we turned bitter at them and made obscene gestures when we were sure they weren't giving us a ride. We stood with our thumbs out and the trucks went by for hours. After a while, even the road seemed bitter. We swore at the drivers under skies I remember the color of winter. I've never been able to tolerate those British war novels that see war as an adhesive force binding us all together in our common cause.

Once I hitchhiked a long way to see a friend. We had been

in training together for over a year in the States. I was well along with my missions and feeling the strain. Each flight seemed tougher as my imagination worked overtime on the danger during the long periods of bad weather when we were grounded. I don't know how many rides it took to get to my friend's base, but when I finally arrived we chatted about old friends in training, who had been killed, who got to stay in the States. I'd made arrangements to be away from the base for a night and stayed over. The next morning I started home. I picked up a ride early in an ammo truck. It was hooded, something like a covered wagon. I yelled "Cerignola" at the driver, he yelled what I heard as "Cerignola" back, and I piled in. The opening in the back was small, and I only glimpsed the landscape as we bounced along the miles. When I got out, I was in a town I'd never seen, miles off-course. Some American fliers were walking about, and I saw one I'd known slightly in training. He told me I was in Spinazzola. Where was Cerignola? He didn't know. Lord, I was lost in the Italian countryside. What if I didn't get back? Would I be court-martialed? I bought a carton of cigarettes in a small PX and started out of town.

Spinazzola is a hill town, and I walked out of it down a long dirt road lined with shade trees. The road ran out before me through hills of grass, and I walked a long time. What if I was scheduled to fly tomorrow and wasn't there? I thumbed the army vehicles that came by and none stopped. I considered lying down in the road to stop someone, but that was no thought to have in those days. Someone might just run over me and keep going. "You should have seen me flatten that fly boy lootenant."

After I'd walked for well over an hour, I sat down to rest by a field of grass. I was tired, dreamy, the way we get without enough sleep, and I watched the wind move in waves of light across the grass. The field slanted and the wind moved uphill across it, wave after wave. The music and motion hypnotized me. The longer the grasses moved, the more passive I became. Had I walked this road when I was a child? Something seemed familiar. I didn't care about getting back to the base now. I didn't care about the war. I was not a part of it anymore.

Trucks went by and I didn't even turn to watch them, let alone
thumb a ride. Let them go. I would sit here forever and watch
the grass bend in the wind and the war would end without me
and I would not go home, ever. Years later in psychoanalysis I
would recount this, and the doctor would explain it as a moment of surrender, when my system could no longer take the
fear and the pressure and I gave up. If that's how to lose a
war, we were wrong to have ever won one. Years after the war,
I would try to do that day justice in a poem and would fail
miserably. I wouldn't even spell "Spinazzola" right, and my
editor wouldn't catch it.

Centuries Near Spinnazola

This is where the day went slack.
It could have been digestion or the line
of elms, the wind relaxed and flowing
and the sea gone out of sight.
This is where the day and I surrendered
as if the air
were suddenly my paramour.

It is far from any home. A white
farm tiny from a dead ten miles
of prairie, gleamed. I stood on grass
and saw the bombers cluster,
and drone the feeble purpose of a giant.

Men rehearsed terror at Sardis
And Xerxes beat the sea.

And prior to the first domestic dog,
a king of marble, copper gods,
I must have stood like that and heard
the cars roar down the road,
the ammo wagon and the truck,
must have turned my back on them
to see the stroke of grass on grass
on grass across the miles of roll,

the travel of my fever now, my urge
to hurt or love released and flowing.

A public yes to war. A Greek will die
and clog the pass to wreck our strategy.
There will be a time for towns to burn
and one more sea to flog into a pond.*

I got a ride shortly after I left the field of waving grass and in a short time was on foot on the outskirts of Canosa. I knew where I was now. Canosa was off-limits, so I couldn't pass through. I had to skirt the town, across barren farm land, and halfway across the field no one had planted for years, I met a woman, perhaps thirty, and her daughter, maybe eight. The woman was dark and beautiful, her face strong, handsome, and brown, her eyes and hair the same heavy black. She wanted me to sell her a pack of cigarettes from the carton I'd bought in Spinazzola and I refused. I still don't know why I didn't give her the carton. What the hell, I could get more. That day haunted me, came back unexpected when I sat in a class, or later when I was at work in the aircraft company, or when I fished or drank in a tavern, came back welcome to remind me how harmonious and peaceful we can feel, came back unwelcome to remind me how we learn little from our positive experiences, how we slip back too easily into this ungenerous world of denial and possession. I've made far worse mistakes than refusing that woman cigarettes, but no mistake came back so often. After being bitten by a dog or stoned by Italian boys my lack of generosity could have been understandable. But after the field of grass? . . .

Do you understand? I'm not sure I do. I had to find the field again. I had to find Spinazzola and retrace that day. If you need a reason, say I am a silly man.

We talked money in the streets of Cerignola, and in a matter of minutes we had a car, a driver, two assistant drivers, all young men, and we were shooting off at far too fast a speed toward Canosa. I wondered if it would be there, Spinaz-

* From *A Run of Jacks* (Minneapolis: Univ. of Minnesota Press, 1961), p. 36. Reprinted with permission of the author.

zola, the road leading out, the field of grass. At least some of it was true: there, to our right as we neared Canosa was the field where I'd made the mistake. Was that woman still lovely? Probably not. Probably fat and lined. Italians let themselves get old as if time were a natural thing. In Canosa, an old man in a horse-drawn wagon blocked the road. Our young driver and his assistants screamed *"cornut' "* as he mumbled bitterly at them and his balky horse.

A few miles later, Spinazzola came at us, riding high on a hilltop and glowing white and gray like a tourist come-on brochure. I always have the same feeling when I see those hill towns: I'll go there and never leave. Yet, from this vantage I couldn't remember it. Did I have the name wrong? Maybe there were two Spinazzolas. But in the town, I recognized it immediately.

My wife and I walked about Spinazzola. Down at the end of the town we found the old dirt road lined with windbreak trees leading downhill away into the uninhabited countryside below. And there, near where the road led out of town, was an old *cantina.* Inside, marvelous, old crude wood tables and benches, warm, dim, comforting light, a friendly old man who offered us *fagiuoli.* But we wanted only wine. Wine, and the feeling one gets in a *cantina,* like you want every friend you ever had to be there with you.

I hope the *cantine* never die in Italy, but I'm sure they are being replaced by the plastic bars with the ugly, expensive chrome coffee machines, the ridiculous pastries that look unique and all taste alike, and the awful excuses for liquor that look like various colored skin astringents sitting in bottles some decadent child designed. We sat there and drank wine, and the *cantina* became very much like that field of grass I still had to find.

I found it. It was a lot farther than I'd remembered and I was surprised I'd walked so far that day nearly twenty years before. It must have been five miles out of town. I saw it just for a moment as we sped by in the car and I didn't ask the driver to stop. I didn't even mention it to my wife at the time, and that was unusual because we were fond of sharing our intimate affections for places. Back in Cerignola, I told her I'd

seen it. It was still there and long ago something, important
only to me, had really happened. Whatever it was, I didn't accept completely the psychoanalyst's explanation of it. It obviously had much truth to it, but it was maybe too pat. Whatever, by now I was old enough to know explanations are
usually wrong. We never quite understand and we can't quite
explain.

Spinazzola: Quella Cantina Là

A field of wind gave license for defeat.
I can't explain. The grass bent. The wind
seemed full of men but without hate or fame.
I was farther than that farm where the road
slants off to nowhere, and the field I'm sure
is in this wine or that man's voice. The man
and this canteen were also here
twenty years ago and just as old.

Hate for me was dirt until I woke up
five miles over Villach in a smoke
that shook my tongue. Here, by accident,
the wrong truck, I came back to the world.
This canteen is home-old. A man can walk
the road outside without a song or gun.
I can't explain the wind. The field is east
toward the Adriatic from my wine.

I'd walked from cruel soil to a trout
for love but never from a bad sky
to a field of wind I can't explain.
The drone of bombers going home
made the weather warm. My uniform
turned foreign where the olive trees
throw silver to each other down the hill.

Olive leaves were silver I could spend.
Say wind I can't explain. That field is vital
and the Adriatic warm. Don't our real friends

tell us when we fail? Don't honest fields
reveal us in their winds? Planes and men
once tumbled but the war went on absurd.
I can't explain the wine. This crude bench
and rough table and that flaking plaster—
most of all the long nights make this home.

Home's always been a long way from a friend.
I mix up things, the town, the wind, the war.
I can't explain the drone. Bombers seemed
to scream toward the target, on the let-down
hum. My memory is weak from bombs.
Say I dropped them bad with shaking sight.
Call me German and my enemy the air.

Clouds are definite types. High ones, cirrus.
Cumulus, big fluffy kind, and if with rain,
also nimbus. Don't fly into them.
I can't explain. Somewhere in a gray ball
wind is killing. I forgot the stratus
high and thin. I forget my field
of wind, out there east between
the Adriatic and my second glass of wine.

I'll find the field. I'll go feeble down
the road strung gray like spoiled wine
in the sky. A sky too clear of cloud
is fatal. Trust the nimbus. Trust dark clouds
to rain. I can't explain the sun. The man
will serve me wine until a bomber fleet
lost twenty years comes droning home.

I can't expain. Outside, on the road
that leaves the town reluctantly,
way out the road's a field of wind.*

* From *Good Luck in Cracked Italian* (New York and Cleveland: World
Publishing, 1969), pp. 43-44. Reprinted with permission of the author.

One down and one to go. Now we would find the air base. Then, my past safely reclaimed, we would become tourists again and move on to Lecce and the baroque churches.

I'd already seen Vincenzo Lattaruolo in the streets of Cerignola the day before. It was a hard face to miss, homely, rough, humane. With his big broken nose and his coarse features, he would be a natural as a character in films. We needed a driver to help us find the airfield, and he offered his services.

When he had been a young boy, maybe ten or eleven, Vincenzo had worked at one of the American air bases. I asked about Pete, also a native of Cerignola, who had worked at ours. Vincenzo said Pete had gone north to Milan to work in the factories. Vincenzo picked up a friend who turned out to be the driver and we went out to find the site of the 825th Squadron, 484th Bomb Group.

It wasn't easy. For two days we ran about the grain-covered countryside and we found the site of many squadrons, but not the 825th. It didn't help when I mentioned it had been located the same place as the group headquarters, and by the third day I was getting discouraged. There had been many squadrons in that region called Tretitoli. Then I remembered the three whores in the pumphouse.

Three whores had set up shop in a pumphouse about a quarter of a mile from the squadron and had operated there for weeks. When the command discovered them, clued by the sudden breakout of VD in the men, it took photos before throwing them out, and pasted the pictures on placards which were posted on the squadron bulletin board. The caption read "The Pumphouse Trio" in big printed letters. Then under the photo of the three wretched-looking creatures, a sarcastic diatribe congratulated the American G.I. on his taste in women. The poor prostitutes looked so scroungy I imagined one might contact VD just looking at the photo.

Italians seem to remember subjects of gossip no matter how old, and Vincenzo picked up as I told him and the driver about the whores. The word for pumphouse was beyond me, but *torre d'acqua* was good enough.

Soon we were approaching the site. The farm buildings

we had used for group headquarters and the squadron mess hall were still intact. My wife knew we had found it, and she murmured, "Oh, dear" and started to cry softly. I never understood how she knew. I'd never described it to her nor had I given any sign of recognition.

There they were. The squadron mess hall on the corner. The courtyard that had been our outdoor theater where Joe Louis, the only celebrity to visit, us, walked through the crowd of G.I.s who were yelling, "Hey, Joe. Want to fight?" and stood on the stage, his huge hands reaching nearly to his knees because his powerful shoulders were so slanted. The group intelligence building. The group commander's upstairs quarters, and below it the briefing room where we would sit very early in the morning and stare at the red ribbon on the map leading to the target. Silence when the ribbon led to Vienna and back (would we get back?), or to Munich, or Linz. Joking if it was a "milk run." More often, than not we heard our fearful silence as we stared at the map and listened to the briefing.

The other buildings were gone, the squadron headquarters, the squadron intelligence building, the sheet-metal quonset hut movie house and theater. Remember the marvelous Italian magician? The Italian jazz band that played famous American numbers and had the solos memorized note for note? Even the drum solo was Krupa, no variation from the original. The movie *Bombardier,* when Pat O'Brien said, "General, you'll see the day when the pilot is only a taxi driver paid to carry the bombardier over the target," and the riot that threatened to start when the pilots in the audience, who worked themselves to exhaustion flying formation for eight and nine hours each mission, began to scream while the bombardiers cheered? What was the name of that even worse movie where Noah Beery, Jr., home with wounds and recuperating on the sands of Santa Monica with Martha O'Driscoll, said with solemnity and resolve, "I can't wait to get another crack at them," and we yelled "Shit," and "Fuck you," and "Oh, my naked ass"? And wasn't that a good build? Martha O'Driscoll's? We whistled and stomped when she came on the screen in her bathing suit.

Beautiful fields of grain now and recently constructed farmhouses nearby, a part of the *Mezzogiorno* program. I showed my wife where our tent had been, and I remembered a subnormal farm boy who brought eggs to sell. We teased him a lot. One of us would say, "New York." And he would say, "New York fineesh." He thought major American cities had been leveled by bombing, and we found his ignorance funny.

Maybe because the day was bright, the grain a warm green in the wind, and the ground hard, I remembered Captain Simmons, the squadron supply officer who didn't provide us with enough blankets, and the cold, wet winter of 1944–45 when we shuddered at night trying to escape into sleep from the cold. I wrote Grandmother and asked for a sleeping bag and she sent one. In 1964 I still had it, somewhere among our belongings back home. Simmons didn't seem to do much but make excuses and bullshit a lot and hate Italians.

A young G.I., maybe nineteen (I was twenty) knocked up a farm girl who lived near the base. Her father demanded the boy marry her and the boy wanted to. But Simmons intervened. "I'm not going to stand by and see that nice kid throw his life away on a goddamn eye-tie." Simmons and some others had gone to the farm to "reason" with the father. I don't know how they communicated with no common language, but Simmons bragged about knocking "the old bastard" around when he insisted on the wedding. "All that son-of-a-bitch wants is to marry his daughter off to an American so they can get in on some of our money," Simmons explained with no self-doubt. A long time later, I knew enough about the southern Italian peasant and the power of religion in that life to realize what a sad business it had been. On bad days, Italians were our enemies.

And it was here where the grain now grew that Squadron Commander Joel O. Moe of North Dakota knocked on each tent door one afternoon and drunkenly announced that he would demonstrate the correct way to slide into third base. No grain then. Only unrelieved mud. And in his fresh uniform, while we stood in front of our tents, Major Joel O. Moe came running down the sloppy road between the two tent rows and hit the mud in what must remain baseball's longest and filthiest slide and we applauded and called him safe.

The mess hall was now a school operated by two nuns who had been little girls in Cerignola during the war. Had they begged me once for candy and cigarettes? They gave us *strega* and cookies and we spent a warm hour there. Later I would try to do the experience justice.

Tretitoli, Where the Bomb Group Was

Windy hunks of light, no prop wash, bend
the green grain no one tried to grow
twenty years ago. Two nuns run a school
where flyers cursed the endless marmalade
and Spam, or choked their powdered eggs
down throats Ploesti tightened in their dreams.
Always phlegm before the engines warmed
and always the private gesture of luck—
touching a bomb, saying the name of a face
spun in without a sound at Odertol.

Hope to win a war gets thin when nuns
pour *strega* in a room where dirty songs
about the chaplain boomed. Recent land reform
gave dirt to the forlorn. That new farm
stands where I would stand in the afternoon
alone and stare across those unfarmed miles
and plan to walk them to the yellow town
away from war, disguised in shepherd black.
That pumphouse hid three whores for weeks
until disease began to show.

Now, no roar. No one sweats the sky out
late in day. No trace of squadron huts
and stone block walls supporting tents.
Those grim jokes. The missions flown
counted on the plane in cartoon bombs.
Always wide awake toward the end
when the man came saying time to fly,

awake from dreams complete with mobs,
thick clubs and slamming syllables of hun
I couldn't understand, trapped behind
cracked glass somewhere deep in Munich
I had never seen, waiting for their teeth
to snip me from the drunken songs of men.

We drive off. Children wait for class.
Grain is pale where truck pools were,
parked planes leaked oil or bombs were piled.
The runway's just a guess. I'd say, there.
Beyond the pumphouse and restricted whores
where nuns and shepherds try to soar by running,
arms stuck out for wings against the air,
and wind is lit in squadrons by the grain.*

Not good enough. I should have given it more time. The last six lines in the third stanza refer to a recurring nightmare I suffered the last weeks before we left for home. That face spun in at Odertol was a young man named Sofio from Chicago, a bombardier, eager to be friends. His pilot's name was Martin, and the crew seemed doomed from the first. They crashed once on takeoff and survived. Another time, separated from the formation in a plane crippled by flak damage, they were hopped by three ME-109 fighters and would not have lived had not four P-51 fighters from the only Negro fighter squadron in the theater of operations shown up to rescue them. Only two of the American planes bothered to attack the Germans. The other two hung back in reserve above a cloud. The blacks were hot pilots, and two were enough to route the Messerschmidts. We watched it from the formation.

Because I was a warm, friendly man (still am, I guess), I was sometimes mistaken for a homosexual. Sofio was warm and friendly, too, and years later when I remembered this, I caught myself wondering if he had been homosexual. I was too sexually naïve to consider those matters when I was twenty. Whatever his sexual leanings, he was a likable young man. He died at Odertol near the Polish border, nailed by centrifugal

*From *Good Luck in Cracked Italian*, pp. 37-38.

force to the interior of a B-24 that would never pull out of the tight spin down five miles of sky. I remember the Messerschmidts shooting into the bomber even after it was hopelessly locked in the spin. I remember my terror that day, the unbelievable number of German fighters that struck during the eight minutes we were left unprotected by our own fighters on the bomb run because those who took us up there for the long haul had to turn back to avoid running short of fuel, and my certainty we would be killed. We had crashed only a week before—miraculously the full load of gas and bombs hadn't ignited. That was our first mission following the crash and it was hardly one to rebuild our confidence. I was so frightened that day that the sight of Martin and crew spinning into oblivion remained immediate and vivid long after the fear was in the past. It is still vivid. Sofio. Why did I think of him that day in 1963 in Tretitoli? I didn't know him well. Maybe because in a world of men he remained, like me, a boy, and I sensed that. Like me, he had not developed the cold exterior expected of men in those times.

Our losses were terrible. The wing must have lost at least 30 percent, the highest we suffered that late in the war. And no publicity because it happened on December 17, 1944, the same day the Battle of the Bulge began.

One German fighter had come into the formation, and instead of shooting and pouring through had put the nose up, like putting on the brakes, and hung in full view like a hesitant bird. Our tail gunner, Tony Cartwright, said it was like a target in a shooting gallery. He, no doubt with help from other gunners in our six-ship box, blew it apart. He speculated that the pilot was a woman, given the timidity of the unexpected and fatal maneuver. We had heard rumors that German women were flying fighters that late in the war. We gave each other congratulations on the ground, loud, wild, laughing congratulations for being alive. We did not mourn those who hadn't come back. We were too happy to have made it ourselves.

I remembered the dark green man from the gunnery shed who had to be flown to Bari for hospitalization. Our co-pilot flew him there. His wife had sent him a "Dear John" letter. He could do nothing about his loss but dwell on it until it was too much and he blew his stomach open with a .45 he had just repaired.

I remembered that only a day or two after we arrived we were called to a meeting of officers in squadron headquarters where we heard the squadron commander deliver an incoherent speech about formation flying. He ended this chaotic diatribe by assuring us that he was a good guy and if any of us would just have a drink with him we'd realize just how good a guy he was. A week later he was sent home, a mental casualty of the war.

I remembered a co-pilot from Tennessee who came into our tent and sobbed because his crew had crashed trying to land in Vis and some were dead. He had stayed behind and claimed that if he'd been there to help the pilot, it would not have happened. And I remembered his pilot when he came back weeks later, his face so disfigured I barely recognized him.

And Charlie Marshall. Sweet, bullshitting Charlie Marshall from Texas. He had some bad luck, a couple of crashes and other narrow escapes. The Germans shot his plane up bad one day over Vienna. By holding the stick back as far as he could he managed to stagger over Yugoslavia and bail everyone out. He came back limping and pale two weeks later, having been rescued by Tito's partisans. His leg was injured in the jump, but he was pale from the slivovitz the partisans forced on him morning to night. He also had had a frightful time talking the partisans out of shooting his co-pilot. Since the co-pilot's name was Gross and since he didn't drink, the partisans suspected he was not an American.

All flying was voluntary. You could quit whenever you wanted and all you lost was your flight pay. We didn't quit because of social pressure, fear of what others would think, and the fear of ending up in the combat ground forces, although that was a remote possibility. Charlie Marshall had had it and he quit. "Hugo," he said to me, "for every man there's a limit. There are pilots with 30,000 hours in the air. They haven't reached their limit. Maybe they never will. But for old Charlie Marshall, it's nineteen hundred and twenty-six hours." He had acquired about 1,700 hours as an instructor before he was transferred to combat.

They threatened Charlie with court-martial, but he knew

his rights and held firm. Finally, they offered to fly him to Naples where he could catch a boat home. "You're not flying Charlie Marshall anywhere," he assured them. How I admired his resolve. Finally, they had to drive him across Italy in a truck. We watched him wave from the truck when it pulled out. He was grinning and very much alive, and I had the feeling he would be very much alive for a long time.

Nothing would do but that we lunch at the home of the driver, Vincenzo's friend. It was a house I'd passed many times on the edge of Cerignola twenty years before. Now: screaming children silenced by screaming parents. Tripe and wine. A long afternoon. Why did you come back? I don't know. Are you still flying? No. No. That was just the war. I'm a poet now. No. Not famous at all. Just one book published. Another taken. Rich? Hardly. What did I do in America? Worked in an aircraft factory. And what do you do? What we can. Drivers sometimes. Drivers, today. No. I will not go back to the aircraft factory. When our money is gone we must go home and find jobs. Yes. Cerignola is much better now. No beggars. No bad odors. Lots of young men. Lots of grain in the fields. And it is all beautiful now, all much better now. That back there, that war. That was a terrible time. *Troppo tensione. Troppo miseria. Troppo fame.*

Vincenzo drove us back to the hotel. Could we stay longer? No, we were taking a bus that afternoon to Bari. I was feeling the wine as we rode through the wide streets of Cerignola.

Reputation? I came from a town with a bad reputation too, just like the reputation Cerignola had in Puglia. What the hell does it mean? Look at the warm, friendly time we had had at lunch, the long afternoon of hospitality. How do nice people get in a war? People like Sofio or Charlie Marshall? How does anyone? Could this be the place we ridiculed and sometimes feared and came to with hard feelings, yelling at children who begged us for food, trying to scare them away? *Troppo miseria* is right. That's what the Neapolitan cabbies say about Naples and that's what I say about the whole damned world. And what the hell can we do about it but hope we are born again, next time better. I didn't know how good the poem would be but it would be honest and I would like it because it wouldn't be any tougher than the human heart needs to be.

April in Cerignola

This is Puglia and cruel. The sun is mean
all summer and the *tramontana*
whips the feeble four months into March.
It was far too tense. Off the streets by five.
Flyers screaming begging children off
and flyers stabbed. The only beauty
is the iron grillwork, and neither that
nor spring was here when I was young.

It used to be my town. The closest one
for bomb-bomb boys to buy *spumante* in.
It reeked like all the towns. Italian men
were gone. The women locked themselves in dark
behind the walls, the bullet holes patched now.
Dogs could sense the madness and went mute.
The streets were mute despite the cry
of children: give me a cigarette. But always flat—
the land in all directions and the time.

I was desolate, too, and so survived.
I had a secret wish, to bring much food
and feed you through the war. I wished
you also dead. All roads lead to none.
You're too far from the Adriatic
to get good wind. Harsh heat and roaring cold
are built in like abandonment each year.
And every day, these mean streets open
knowing there's no money and no fun.

So why return? You tell me I'm the only one
came back, and you're amazed
I haven't seen Milan. I came in August
and went home in March, with no chance
to experience the miles of tall grain
jittering in wind, the olive trees
alive from recent rain. You're still my town.
The men returned. The women opened doors.
The hungry lived and grew, had children

they can feed. Most of all, the streets are wide,
lead nowhere, and dying in your weather
takes a lifetime of surviving last year's war.*

At the hotel when we got out, Vincenzo did too. He said,
"Of all the Americans here during the war, you're the only one
who ever returned." He started to sob and he suddenly em-
braced me and said, *"Come mio fratello."* His crying became
more violent and I turned, vaguely embarrassed, and started
up the stairs, his choked sobs trailing me from the street. "Oh,
hell," I thought, "I'll never be Humphrey Bogart or Herbert
Marshall," and I sat down on the stairs and had a good cry too.

My wife sat understanding beside me while I blubbered,
matched Vincenzo Lattaruolo sob for strangulated sob, though
he was hidden from me beyond the closed door, and I never
saw him again. I still wasn't sure why I'd come back, but I felt
it must be the best reason in the world.

* From *Good Luck in Cracked Italian,* pp. 35–36.

9

How Poets
Make a Living

QUESTION: You worked for thirteen years in the real world before you went into academia? What are the differences for a poet?

I dread that question, but by now I've developed some replies the audience might find funny. How do you answer it seriously? I hate that phrase "the real world." Why is an aircraft factory more real than a university? Is it? In universities I've had in my office ex-cons on parole, young people in tears racked with deep sexual problems, people recently released from mental hospitals, confused, bewildered, frightened, hoping, with more desperation than some of us will ever be unlucky enough to know, that they will remain stable enough to stay in school, and out of hospitals forever. I've seen people so forlorn that I've sat there praying as only an unreligious man can pray that I don't say something wrong, that I can spare their feelings, that I might even say something that will make their lives easier if only for a few moments. Sad drug addicts too. Not people you usually meet in industrial offices. Often they are coming to me because I'm a poet and I'm supposed to be wise, to have some secret of existence I can pass on to the forlorn. In some ways the university is a far more real world than business.

So there are differences, but I'm not sure they affect the writing of poems, though obviously they matter one hell of a lot to me. I'm more inclined to wonder what difference it makes what a poet does for a living, or how he leads his life. Sometimes these preoccupations can become absurd.

I have here a book by a Llewelyn Powys, called *Advice to a Young Poet*, The Bodley Head, London, 1949. You needn't read far until you run into:

> (1) To be a poet you must live with an intensity five times, nay a hundred times more furiously than that of those about you. There is no scene, no experience which should not contribute to your poetic appreciations and culture.
>
> (2) You must regulate your life as strict as a religious devotee. You must keep a strict eye on your health. Live healthy. Though you go in rags be careful every day to wash every inch of your body so it is always beautiful and *fresh*—even if you are too hard up to afford extravagant washing bills, wash your underclothes with your own hand as though this extra personal fastidiousness were part of a religious rite. Never use powder or scent under any circumstances. In your eating keep as far as possible from animal foods, eat dairy produce, fruit, and vegetables. Always sleep with your windows wide open. Always try to take natural exercise. Aim at getting up half an hour earlier than other people and walking if possible to catch a glimpse of the sea *every morning*. These walks should be very important to gaining a heightened consciousness of existence. The senses are most keen and receptive at such a time. Do the same if possible in the evening, sending your soul from your wrist like a Merlin hawk to fly to the stars, or to ride upon the wind or shiver in the rain above the housetops.

That seems silly in print, and in life it can get boring. I've been seriously advised to take drugs, to avoid drugs, to eat only seafood, to live on welfare, to stop drinking (good advice it turned out), to drink more (at one time an impossibility), to avoid sex, to pursue sex, to read philosophy, to avoid philosophy. Once someone told me I should master every verse form known to man. A poet is seldom hard up for advice. The worst part of it all is that sometimes the advice is coming from other poets, and they ought to know better.

But the question has been asked about the differences between the business world and academia. And because it doesn't deserve a serious answer, I'm perverse enough to give a few from there (business) and here (university).

There: 62,000 employees and no one cares that I write poems.

Here: When I first start, twenty-six employees in the department and three of them hate me because I write poems.

There: Those who know I write poems don't seem to assume anything is special about me.

Here: I've been named the head of a student dope ring. A student informant tells the administration I've advised students to print and distribute copies of a "dirty poem" about the campus. I am a homosexual. I am a merciless womanizer. I throw wild parties. I write my poems in Italian and then translate them into English. I come to class dressed in dirty, torn T-shirts. I am a liberal, a reactionary, a communist, a Nazi.

There: When you leave at the end of eight hours, there's a tendency to feel you've fulfilled your obligation to the universe. Why go home and write?

Here: When teaching well I'm making love to a room of people. Is that the same energy that goes into a poem? Is that meeting my obligation? Is the day over now? See. I'm a victim too.

I'm apt to sound too self-assured about the unimportance of a poet's job because no matter what I've done for a living I've gone on writing, and because with one exception I've never found the initiating subject of a poem where I worked. That one exception I didn't see myself, but rather heard about from an immediate superior.

C was easy to dislike if you saw only his surface. He was humorless and seemed to have no friends, and he tried to be what he thought big business wanted its executives to be. He hid his emotions under a mask of self-control. His upper lip had vertical creases from years of pursing his mouth in what would appear to be considered objective thought.

Once he confided to me that he found democracy wanting because the vote of each person in the shops who didn't have the prestigious position he had and who hadn't made money in outside investments as he had counted the same as his vote in an election. Another time he called a black who worked in our office "Rastus" aloud in a meeting. By then I knew him well. When he said Rastus he was actually trying to be funny and informal, to include the black rather than ridicule him. He was in fact a decent man, but he had practiced inhumanity so long that when he tried to be human he was crude.

He was obsessed with success. Once he told me about a man who was offered a bonus of a million dollars to take a position with a large industrial firm. A few weeks later, half-drunk on martinis at lunch, he told me *he* had been offered that million dollars to take that job. I didn't think he believed it, but he wanted to say it about himself. And typically, while he had spent years repressing his warmth, he had also developed ways of gaining the emotional advantage. (Whoever described the bourgeois as an emotional politician knew what he was talking about.) Once I brought him something to sign and thinking he had no pen, I offered him mine. He said coldly, "I have my own, thank you," and pulled it out from his inside jacket pocket. Even though he knew me well, he couldn't stop himself from chalking up another victory.

One day in his office he started chatting about a distasteful job he once had as one of a small group of men who were assigned to evicting a squatter from company land at Plant I. Plant I was the first and, for a long time, the only Boeing plant. It was on the bank of the Duwamish River, between the river and the Duwamish slough where, as a boy, I'd fished for porgies. Later the slough was filled in.

Plant I was now a small facility. They developed a gas-turbine engine there for trucks and cars but never could get the price down to compete with conventional car motors. Plant II, the Developmental Center, Renton, these had become the centers of activity. Plant I, once a narrow hope for the unemployed during the Depression, was now all but forgotten. A few minor machine shops, some draftsmen and engineers, a couple of labs. Whenever I went there it seemed to me a welcome relief from the bursting, profitable huge factories and offices of Plant II. Even the forlorn drabness of it was attractive. Compared with the rest of the company it seemed almost pastoral.

The company owned the land, nearly all of it, right up to the river, or rather where the river swelled to when high tides in the bay two miles downstream backed up. Naturally, when the plant was fenced, part of the property remained outside the fence. The fence had to be straight for practical reasons, and the river bank was serrated with coves and juttings. On the northeast point of the property sticking out into the river and outside the fenced boundary, a squatter lived with his wife. They had a shell of a house, four walls and a roof, doorless doorways and no partitioning walls inside. No windows. No floors. No running water or electricity. And no one remembered how that shell or that squatter came to be there, but part of the house was on company land. It couldn't be moved back or it would fall into the river.

The squatter was a small man, and he and his wife never bathed. His wife, perhaps twenty years younger, always had on rubber boots. They hauled water in buckets from a gas station about three blocks away. When they walked along the trail just outside the fence, between the fence and the river, the Boeing guards would taunt the man, and he would jump up and down in violent anger and scream back wild, incoherent phrases. He dominated his wife something awful, ordering her about like a slave. And she obeyed every command.

They had been living there for about five years. Under state law, two more years and they'd have legal ownership of the land. The company had plans for the property, so they started eviction action.

As C talked, a picture started to form. The squatter, evidently insane, frightened, even terrified at the idea of moving. The woman, totally dependent, probably masochistic, maybe subnormal. What also fascinated me was C. I could sense his complicated feelings. He was troubled by the man even after all these years because the man was so irredeemably outside any values my boss assumed normal. He was regretful because he had been assigned to the eviction and so was partly responsible for throwing those sad people out. And secretly, even to himself secretly, he admired, almost envied, the man because the man was not civilized, and I suppose basically no one wants to be civilized. In his own way, C was civilized and at what a price.

The poem almost wrote itself. After it had been accepted by *The Yale Review,* but before it was published, I transferred to the Renton plant, said good-bye to C and hello to another boss. Changes of that kind were normal at Boeing. Treat those who work for you well, tomorrow you'll be working for them, we used to say.

When the poem was published I showed it to someone at work, and before long several people in the office at Renton heard about it. It turned out many of them had been at Plant I at the time of the eviction, and they remembered it vividly. Especially they remembered the strange man and woman who were evicted. They all wanted a copy of the poem, so I kept sending away for copies of the magazine. Never have so many copies of *The Yale Review* found their way into the Boeing Company. I included the poem in my second book, *Death of the Kapowsin Tavern.*

The Squatter on Company Land

We had to get him off, the dirty elf—
wild hair and always screaming at his wife
and due to own our land in two more years—
a mud flat point along the river
where we planned our hammer shop.
Him, his thousand rabbits, the lone goat
tied to his bed, his menial wife: all out.

To him, a rainbow trail of oil might mean
a tug upstream, a boom, a chance a log
would break away and float to his lasso.
He'd destroy the owners' mark and bargain
harshly with the mill. He'd weep and yell
when salmon runs went by, rolling
to remind him he would never cheat the sea.

When did life begin? Began with running
from a hatchet some wild woman held,
her hair a gray cry in alfalfa
where he dug and cringed? Began in rain
that cut the light into religious shafts?
Or just began the way all hurt begins—
hit and dropped, the next man always righteous
and the last one climbing with a standard tongue?

In his quick way, swearing at us pressed
against the fence, he gathered rags and wood
and heaped them in the truck and told his wife
"Get in," and rode away, a solid glare
that told us we were dying in his eye.*

It was a good thing I wrote the poem when I did. The people at Renton who saw it brought me so many more facts and stories that my imagination could never have handled it all. I would have needed years to forget the details in order to create.

The squatter had worn a yachting cap, and the employees called him The Admiral. I'd made one good guess. The man had kept rabbits, but not nearly a thousand as the poem says. I didn't know why the company wanted the land but I said "hammer shop" because the rhythm seemed to ask for it. Actually they planned a sand-blast facility. "The lone goat" came from two goats I'd seen tied to a kitchen stove in an adobe whorehouse on the outskirts of Juarez on Christmas Day, 1943. Most of the rest is imagination, although salmon did come up the Duwamish River and did roll along the surface, and you could sell stray logs to mills if you found one floating that was unmarked by an owner.

D had been in charge of the eviction team, and he was now there at Renton. He was a far cry from C who had first told me the story. D had repressed none of his humanity in the years he had spent in industry. The eviction, and The Admiral and his wife, had made such an impression on him that

* From *Death of the Kapowsin Tavern* (New York: Harcourt, Brace & World, 1965), p. 49. Reprinted with permission of the author.

even then, almost twenty years later, he still kept the entire
file with him in his desk. He had me to his office several times
(at Boeing your own office meant you were somebody) to talk
about The Admiral. And he talked about The Admiral with
unqualified love.

He showed me aerial photos of the land, the point jutting
out into the river beyond the confines of the rectangular fenc-
ing. And he showed me the following two letters written by
The Admiral. All thanks to some heroic secretary who took
hours to type these from near-illegible, primitive scrawl so I
could have copies. I'm ashamed to admit that over the many
years I've forgotten her name.

Mr. D.
Head of Boeing Co. No. 1
6-1 ave. So.
Seattle, Washington
Dear Mr. D.:
I have seen the way you people straightened. You don't
even come out to where you said it come to. I know a lot
of more than you thought I did. You bought my lawyer but
you're not buying me. You are not owning me. There is
one person and he knows of all things of what men do on
the earth. You did me a lot of harm but there's one thing,
thank God I'm away from your outfit, as far as the poor
man that has to work for your company. I feel sorry for
them. Sure fine to see little people be pushed around but
some day this war will come to an end and your outfit will
be forgotten. You've scured a lot of help and a lot of mis-
fedings amongst right out in the street. I know more about
your outfit than you think. This country was built for more
than one man to enjoy. Thank God there was one dictator
that passed over the hill. You may be making millions of
dollars but there will be a day when you won't be. I am
still suffering from some of your dirty work. I know kind of
man you are and the rest of your so-called class. I don't like
white collared folks very well. I've mostly been with Navajo
Indians and Mexicans when I was a kid amongst the
Eskimos. All this I can prove. I can remember when your

planes went down in the Bay. We got all the news in
Alaska. I was there six years with my father for the Board
of Education. These so-called four lawyers on those phony
bunch of papers you served me. The rest were appointed.
Only one was a lawyer. It is fine when you have everything
in your hands but try and make people like it. Remember
there will be a day for such people of your kind. My fore-
fathers didn't fight for their country to be pushed around.
Our boys are not fighting for Boeings.

Mr. D.: I want you to understand this is what I mean there
is two people involved in this deal. This afternoon you said
this material I take off this house at my risk. I do not want
it damaged because it do not belong to me. I consulted
with these people before I saw you. I know what a man can
do. It is true that I am leaving some things behind. When we
are in transportation at my risk I do not want anything.
I'll start moving as soon as I get the trailer. I knowed I was
ten feet on your ground but possession is nine points in
law. The Welfare told me about the conversation which
you and them have. I got very wet. This morning I'm supposed to get from your Company that will be returned to
my mother. The other concern is Sears & Roebuck. You
better take it easy I said in your office. I know what a
bunch of people can do a house because the day until the
15th is very short. I want to go to get away about as bad as
you want me to get away. Could you let me have a little
electricity to take off this roof—a long extension cord. I
admit I'm on your ground and I'll be just as happy to get
off of it.

A. R. McCollister

When a man is in the middle of the road I can give a man
a drink of water and feed a man. I have done. I only lost
homes in my lifetime. These rabbit hutches I'm taking with
me and other planks that is loose and lumber. I will have
to unbolt the planks to the rabbit house unless you give me
a good price for them like you said this afternoon. That
money will go to my mother. The Welfare will not advance any until the 15th of the month but I'm going to

have the trailer before that. If I had only known what they
was like a day or two ago things might have been different
because I do play around, Mr. D., but a poor man has to
do the best he can.

You can almost smell the man's fear in the words. What an
act of courage it must have been writing these. How little that
poor twisted man had, and a terrifying billion-dollar corporation was taking it away. And what sudden bursts of eloquence
reserved usually it seems for primitives. "I only lost homes in
my lifetime." T .S. Eliot said "Bad poets imitate. Good poets
steal." If not stealing that line means I'm a bad poet, so be it.
I couldn't do it, though years later I changed it to use in a
long poem called "Last Words From Maratea": "Green in your
lifetime/You lost nothing but homes."

As for The Admiral and his wife, their departure was
something like it is in the poem. The Admiral claimed he
owned property in the Monroe Valley, north and somewhat
east of Seattle, about thirty miles away. The company provided
a truck and driver, and in a scene that must have been agoniz-
ing, The Admiral threw worthless things onto the truck, old
pieces of dirty rags, hunks of wood, maybe even stones, anything that might show a hostile world that he was not destitute, that he had the pride of possession still. No one mentioned what became of the rabbits.

The driver drove The Admiral and his wife and their
strange possessions to the Monroe Valley. There for hours The
Admiral directed the driver to this place and that. Is this it?
Yes. No. Wait. That's not it. Down the road farther. I think
this is it. Finally at nine or after, the driver, tired and hungry,
simply announced: This is it. He left The Admiral, his wife,
and the odd items, worthless except in The Admiral's mind,
by the side of a remote country road in the dark. That was the
last anyone I knew ever heard of them.

Although it didn't impress me at the time, it seems important now that no one at Boeing questioned the writing of the
poem. It seemed an unstated fact that people like The Admiral and conditions like eviction are what prompt poems. It
was the only time a lot of people I didn't know at Boeing

were aware I was a poet, and certainly the first time they'd read a poem I'd written. I was surprised at the response, the sophisticated reception. I'm not saying Boeing didn't have its share of Philistines. All groups do. I'm saying that there's a broader base to humanity than I'd been aware of.

I suppose I haven't done anything but demonstrated how I came to write a poem, shown what turns me on, or used to, and how, at least for me, what does turn me on lies in a region of myself that could not be changed by the nature of my employment. But it seems important (to me even gratifying) that the same region lies untouched and unchanged in a lot of people, and in my innocent way I wonder if it is reason for hope. Hope for what? I don't know. Maybe hope that humanity will always survive civilization.

But the original question remains even though I've tried to answer it and some other question it implies. Let's drop the phrase "as a poet." As a person, I simply like teaching in a university better than working in an aircraft factory. The rumors have stopped. The three people who hated me for being a poet have moved on, and the remaining ones know I lead a rather solitary life, certainly not a swinging one. Here, I am close to poetry's only consistent audience. I like students because they are not far removed from being children, and that is a bond between us. What adult would dream of writing a poem? And teaching gives me a personal satisfaction no other job ever did.

But no job accounts for the impulse to find and order those bits and pieces of yourself that can come out only in the most unguarded moments, in the wildest, most primitive phrases we shout alone at the mirror. And no job modifies that impulse or destroys it. In a way The Admiral speaks for all poets, maybe for all people, at least a lot of us. We won't all disappear on a remote country road in the Monroe Valley, but like The Admiral and his wife we are all going into the dark. Some of us hope that before we do we have been honest enough to scream back at the fates. Or if we never did it ourselves, that someone, derelict or poet, did it for us once in some euphonic way our inadequate capacity for love did not deny our hearing.